GEORGIA BONESTEEL'S
Spinning Spools
SAMPLER

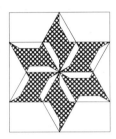

©1992 by Oxmoor House, Inc.
Book Division of Southern Progress Corporation
P.O. Box 2463, Birmingham, Alabama 35201

Published in cooperation with Leisure Arts.

Library of Congress Catalog Number: 92-62899
ISBN: 0-8487-1158-0
Manufactured in the United States of America
First Printing 1992

Editor-in-Chief: Nancy J. Fitzpatrick
Senior Crafts Editor: Susan Ramey Wright
Senior Editor, Editorial Services: Olivia Wells
Director of Manufacturing: Jerry Higdon
Art Director: James Boone

GEORGIA BONESTEEL'S SPINNING SPOOLS SAMPLER

Editor: Carol Cook Hagood
Assistant Editor: Karen Broun Brookshaw
Designer: Diana Smith Morrison
Editorial Assistant: Patricia Weaver
Copy Chief: Mary Jean Haddin
Copy Editor: Susan Smith Cheatham
Production Manager: Rick Litton
Associate Production Manager: Theresa L. Beste
Production Assistant: Pam Beasley Bullock
Photographer: John O'Hagan
Artists: Karen Tindall Tillery, Samuel L. Baldwin, Larry Hunter

Contents

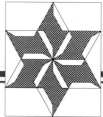

Introduction

The blocks I teach in my seventh Lap Quilting with Georgia Bonesteel PBS series are from Georgia Bonesteel's Spinning Spools: A Pattern Club for Quilters, an exciting collection of patterns old and new. Quilters across the country enjoy receiving this publication in the mail. Each month, shipments of six quilt patterns— complete with cut-and-use plastic templates, full quilt instructions, and a club newsletter—arrive at every member's door. Month by month, members collect club materials in sturdy, colorful three-ring binders.

The quilts from which Spinning Spools patterns are taken show the breathtaking range of the quilter's art. Some are museum pieces; others are treasured family quilts. I have personally designed many patterns for the club, often reaching back to my earliest quilts. Some projects just could not fit into my books, but found a home in the club. Still others are intriguing new designs contributed by quilters throughout the nation. In the Spinning Spools program, we include photographs of some of these memorable quilts, colored drawings of all, and stories about the quiltmakers. Although space does not permit us to include all those materials here, the Spinning Spools Sampler is a good way to bring you a sampling of the quilt blocks, small projects, and quilt designs that appear in the Spinning Spools program. Here you'll find printed patterns for blocks I teach on Lap Quilting with Georgia Bonesteel VII, plus instructions for the Sweet-Gum Chair Pocket, Fan Fire Screen, and three quilts: Spinning Spools Star, Pomegranates, and Georgia's Club Sandwich — an exciting sampler.

Choose Your Favorite Block--or Make Them All!

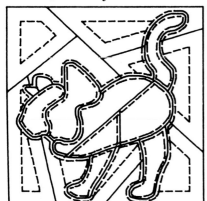

Sampler quilts are composed of different blocks, usually of the same size. The Club Sandwich quilt (page 62) has an even more challenging theme. It's made up not only of different blocks, but of different *size* blocks. Choose twenty of the blocks from this booklet and join them together in this special sampler. (You may want to include other quilt blocks you already have on hand.) The challenge is to bring the different-sized blocks together into four long, vertical rows of five blocks each. By adding spacer borders and pieced Flying Geese segments, you can unify the blocks and build each row up to an 18" width. Then join the four rows together for an unusual and striking sampler quilt.

Keep in mind, too, that each of the block patterns can be used alone to make a quilt.

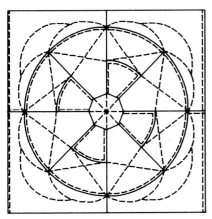
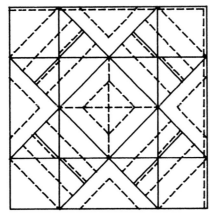

Simply repeat the single design for as many blocks as you need or alternate pieced blocks with blocks of quilting.

In choosing patterns, consider your skill level. The small spool beneath each pattern title contains a 1, 2, or 3. Beginners will find the patterns marked 1 most suitable for first attempts at quilting. Intermediate-level patterns are marked with a 2. Patterns marked with a 3 require the greatest skill or commitment of time.

Make the Templates

Use the geometric and appliqué patterns in this booklet to make quilt templates--the essential tools you'll use to cut out fabric shapes for your quilt. In the past, templates were often made of cardboard, but today there are smarter choices. Quilter's plastic (plain or gridded) is a durable template material that offers firm edges to trace around. Since plastic templates are transparent, it's easy to position them on fabric to use the fabric print to the best advantage. Trace pattern shapes onto the plastic with an indelible pen, using a ruler for the straight lines and a flexicurve for the curved lines. Mark the grain lines and the turning dots that indicate the ¼" seam allowance. Cut out the plastic templates with paper scissors or a rotary cutter and a ruler. Then punch out the turning dots with an ⅛" hole punch.

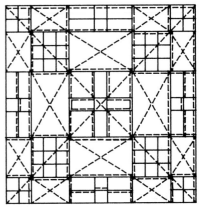

Another smart choice for templates is Grid-Grip™, a gridded paper with a poly-coated backing. Grid-Grip shapes adhere to fabric when pressed with a warm iron. If you cut the Grid-Grip templates finished sized (without the seam allowances) and leave them in place on the fabric pieces until the block is sewn, these handy paper templates will stabilize bias edges and provide a sewing guide as you stitch. Then you can simply peel them off and reuse them many times.

Whatever material you use, accuracy in tracing is essential, since the template will serve as your guide to precision patchwork.

Mark the Fabric and Cut Out the Pieces

Fabric for quiltmaking should be washed, dried, and pressed before using. For best results, use 100% cotton or cotton blends, avoiding the selvage. Save the silks,

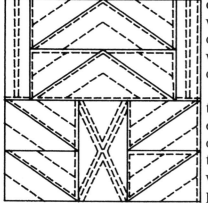

corduroys, wools, and other fabrics for wall hangings or garments.

Use your templates with either scissors or a rotary cutter. To work with scissors, position the template on the fabric (doubled or folded for cutting out multiples), matching the grain line on the template to the crosswise or straight-of-grain of the fabric. (This placement will prevent unstable bias on the outside edges of the completed block.) Trace around the template with a pencil, sliver of

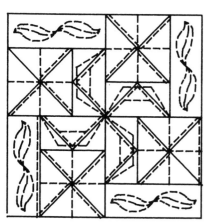

soap, or a chalk wheel. When possible, butt the edges of the marked pieces to save time and fabric. A lapboard covered with sandpaper provides a good non-slip surface on which to do your marking. Cut out fabric pieces with the scissors, turn pieces to the wrong side, and mark turning dots through the punched holes of the template.

Use the rotary cutter with a mat board and thick see-through ruler. Work standing up to provide proper leverage. Layer your

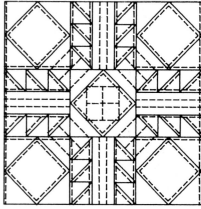

fabric; four layers should be the maximum. Position your template on the fabric and place the ruler on top of the template, letting your fingers fall off the opposite edge of the ruler to aid in anchoring it securely on the fabric. Cut out the shape with the rotary cutter, taking care not to cut into the edge of the plastic template. If you are using finished-size Grid-Grip templates, position the edge of the gridded see-through ruler ¼" from the paper edge to create the correct seam allowance.

For some patterns, in which sets of triangles are repeatedly joined into squares, quick-piecing techniques may be indicated. See Mother's Dream (page 30) for details.

Assemble the Block and Press

Stitch the fabric pieces together to form the patchwork block, following the block assembly instructions for each pattern.

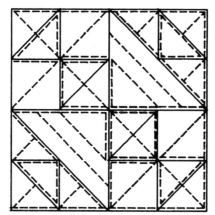

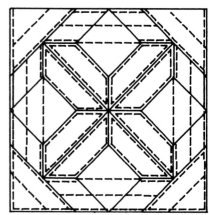

Always start with the smallest pieces and build to larger sections. Note that in some patterns, it's important to leave certain seam allowances unstitched; in some assembly diagrams, circles indicate points at which you should sew just to the ¼" mark, stop, and reverse to lock the stitches in place.

For patterns built from repeated units, you may find it helpful to use the assembly-line technique. Make a stack of similar pieces to be sewn together and run them through the sewing machine one after another, leaving just a short space with a "kite tail" of machine stitches between the sets of pieces. When all the sets have been sewn, clip them apart and move to the next stage of piecing.

Press sections as you go to direct the closed seams in the proper direction (toward the darker fabric, when possible.) Check the accuracy of your ¼" seams by using a master template, cut the correct size for that section of the block (including seam allowances on

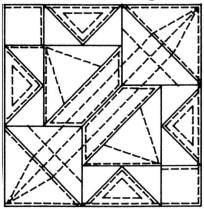

the outer edges). If the pieced section is too small, you are taking too large a seam allowance, causing the block to "shrink." If the section needs to be "pruned" or trimmed, you are taking too small a seam allowance. In this case, the blocks will "grow" (and you will lose the points off pieced stars when blocks are sewn together).

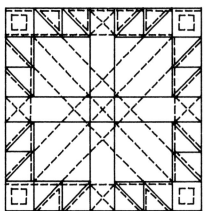 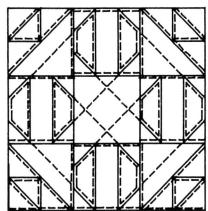 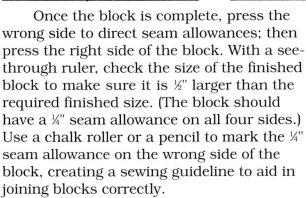

Once the block is complete, press the wrong side to direct seam allowances; then press the right side of the block. With a see-through ruler, check the size of the finished block to make sure it is ½" larger than the required finished size. (The block should have a ¼" seam allowance on all four sides.) Use a chalk roller or a pencil to mark the ¼" seam allowance on the wrong side of the block, creating a sewing guideline to aid in joining blocks correctly.

Decide on the Quilt Layout or Setting

The Club Sandwich sampler quilt is composed of five sampler blocks in four long

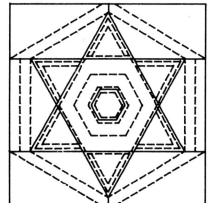

vertical rows. When you have pieced twenty blocks, place them in rows and play with their placement, turning and shifting blocks around to achieve the best effect. Plan rectangular or Flying Geese segments to bring each row to an 18" width. Measure the bed on which you will use the quilt. If the measurement of your bed suggests it, you may want to make each row wider or narrower to increase or decrease the size of the finished quilt. Record your plan in a graph-paper sketch to serve as a sewing guide for placement of blocks and border additions.

Consider other options for the blocks, such as turning them on point, repeating one block throughout, or combining patchwork blocks with plain quilted squares.

Plan the Quilting

The quilting design is an important element in creating the overall character of your finished piece; the play of highlights and shadows created by the quilted line will bring your quilt to life. Decide whether you would like a *compatible* quilting design (one that follows and reinforces the pieced design lines) or a *contrary* design (one that sets up a new design apart from that created by the patchwork lines). The quilting designs we suggest for the Club Sandwich blocks in this booklet, shown here with dashed lines, offer examples of both types of quilting.

Mark the quilting pattern you've chosen on the quilt top with a fabric pen or pencil, a sliver of soap, water-erasable pen, soap-

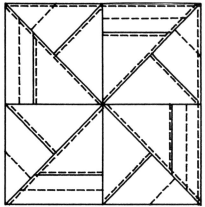

stone marker, or tailor's chalk. Test to make sure that the marker you choose can be easily removed from the fabric you are using. For straight-line quilting, you can place strips of narrow masking tape on your quilt top (once it has been basted) to serve as a temporary marker.

The Quilt Connection

Once the quilt top is marked, make the quilt "sandwich" by assembling the three layers of quilt top, batting, and backing. Baste the layers together with rows of long stitches, cross-hatched about 6" apart.

fluffier the batting, the longer the stitch.

The backing fabric should be easy to needle. Muslin is a popular backing fabric; it highlights the quilting stitches and is inexpensive. A print backing is a good choice for beginners as it does not show-case learner's stitches as prominently as muslin or a dark fabric would.

With the fabric sandwich complete, hand or machine-quilt the piece. Finish the quilt edges with bias binding.

For lap quilting, the quilt should be assembled and quilted in sections, leaving at least ½" unquilted at inside connecting seams. To join the sections together to make the entire quilt, make lap-quilting *connections*. Place edges of the top layer of two sections with right sides facing and join with a ¼" seam. Butt the batting layers together, trimming away excess batting as necessary.

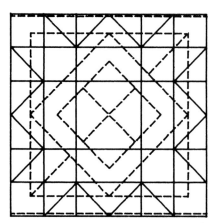
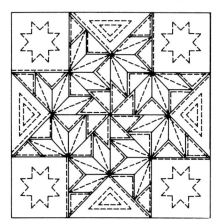
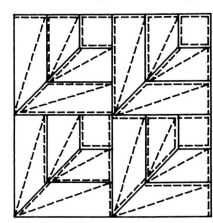

From the many types of batting available today, choose the type that best suits your needs. Polyester or perfected cotton batting can be *high-loft* (fluffy) or *low-loft* (flatter and more compact). Polyester batting need not be quilted as closely as the traditional cotton batting, since it will not separate and get lumpy with washing. There is a direct correlation between the loft of the batting and the quilting stitch length. The thinner the batting, the smaller the stitch; the

Turn under the seam allowance of the backing of one section and slipstitch it to the backing of the second section. A print backing will help camouflage lap quilting connections on the back of the quilt.

Don't forget to sign and date your quilt with a fine-point indelible pen or with embroidery stitches. Stay warm!

Georgia Bonesteel

Spinning Spools Blocks

The quilt block patterns offered in
the Spinning Spools Pattern Club reflect
the tremendous variety of American quilt design.
In the following sampling of blocks from
the club program, you'll find
geometric piecework and picture-block
appliqué, traditional and contemporary designs,
flowers and animals, Biblical designs,
and designs reflecting the pioneer experience.
Put them together and
you'll have the makings of a fabulous
Spinning Spools sampler quilt.

Bear's Paw

1 *The Bear's Paw quilt block is an American classic. With its four large, perfectly balanced squares surrounded by a ring of sharp, claw-like triangles, it is at once as sturdy and as feisty as the old grizzly for which it might be named.*

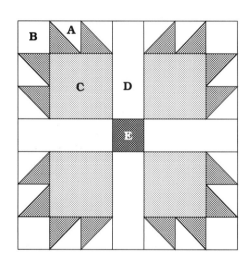

Block

FINISHED SIZE:
12" square

TYPE:
Nine-patch

TEMPLATES:
5 (A-E)

PIECES PER BLOCK:
45

Triangle A:	16 medium gray
	16 white
Square B:	4 white
Square C:	4 light gray
Rectangle D:	4 white
Square E:	1 dark gray

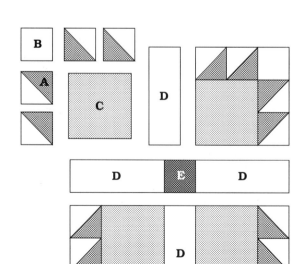

BLOCK ASSEMBLY:

Join each medium gray triangle A to a white triangle A to make A/A squares. (Here's another perfect place to use the quick-piecing techniques I teach in my books.)

Join 2 medium gray/white A/A squares together and add a white square B. Join 2 more A/A squares together and join to a C. Join A/A/A/A/B unit to A/A/A/A/C unit to make a single paw. Join 2 paws together with strip D to make upper section of block. Join 2 more paws together with a strip D for lower section of block.

Make a central strip from D, E, D. Use this strip to join upper and lower sections of block.

Large patterns are for 12" block. Small, gray
patterns are for 6" block.

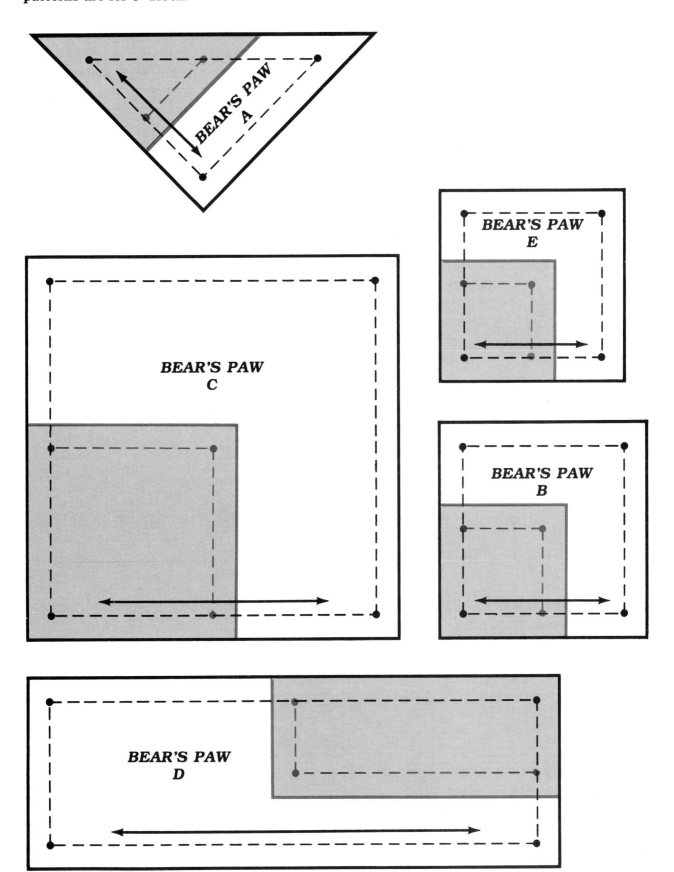

BEAR'S PAW
A

BEAR'S PAW
E

BEAR'S PAW
C

BEAR'S PAW
B

BEAR'S PAW
D

Burgoyne Surrounded

2 *The surrender of the British general John Burgoyne at the Battle of Ticonderoga on October 17, 1777 was the first great American military victory. Many historians believe that this event marked the turning point of the Revolutionary War. Burgoyne Surrounded is a motif that appears in both early American woven coverlets and in quilts to express a patriotic pride.*

Block

FINISHED SIZE:
15" square

TYPE:
Nine-patch

TEMPLATES:
5 (A–E)

PIECES PER BLOCK:
97

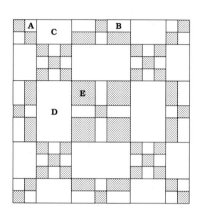

One-color version:

Square A:	33 light gray
	28 white
Rectangle B:	8 light gray
	12 white
Rectangle C:	8 white
Rectangle D:	4 white
Square E:	4 light gray

Two-color version:

Square A:	21 dark gray
	12 light gray
	28 white
Rectangle B:	8 light gray
	12 white
Rectangle C:	8 white
Rectangle D:	4 white
Square E:	4 dark gray

BLOCK ASSEMBLY:

Use template A to make 4 Units 1 and 4 Units 3. Use templates A and B to make 4 Units 2. Use templates A, B, and E to make 1 Unit 4.

Piece units made, along with rectangles C and D, into vertical rows as shown. Join vertical rows.

Note: For one-color version, cut all gray pieces from a single color. For two-color version, cut dark gray pieces in block assembly diagram from one color (such as berry red) to represent Burgoyne's surrounded troops. Cut light gray pieces in diagram from a second color (like indigo) to represent the American forces.

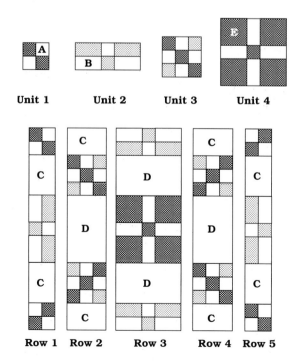

10

Patterns are for 15" block.

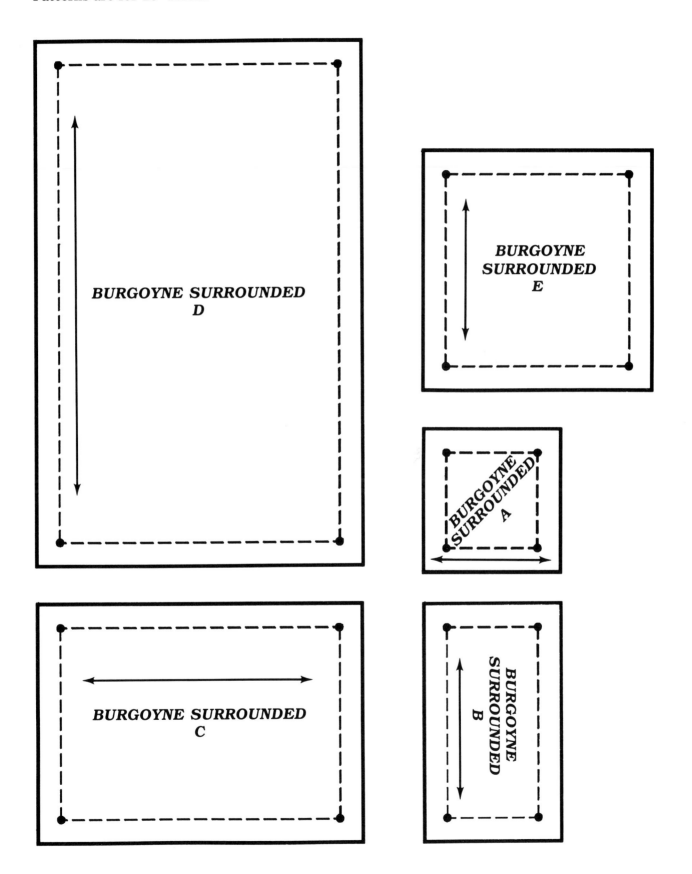

Crazy Cats

2 *Based on Doug Marmee's design Cats Rampant, this appliquéd cat block comes out of the tradition of crazy quilts. First a background square is randomly pieced; then the cat is pieced and appliquéd. If you choose to work with heavier fabrics—wools and corduroys—tie rather than quilt the piece.*

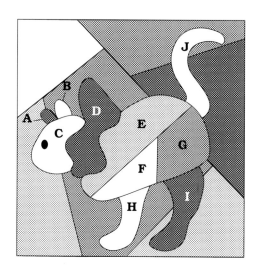

Block

FINISHED SIZE:
10" square

TYPE:
Appliqué

TEMPLATES:
10 (A-J)

PIECES PER BLOCK:
10 plus pieced foundation block

Shapes A, D, I (1 each):	dark gray
Shapes B, C, F, H, J (1 each):	white
Shape E:	light gray
Shape G:	medium gray

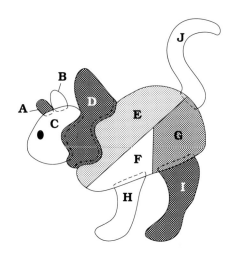

BLOCK ASSEMBLY:

Crazy-piece 10" (plus seam allowances) foundation block.

Piece cat body: Join F and G; then join F/G unit to E.

Pin all appliqué pieces in place, tucking edges of A, B, H, I, and J under C or E/F/G, and tucking edges of C and E/F/G under D. Appliqué shapes A, B, H, I, and J, leaving edges shown as broken lines unturned and unstitched. Then appliqué shapes C and E/F/G, again leaving broken lines unstitched. Finally, appliqué shape D, finishing all edges. Embroider eye.

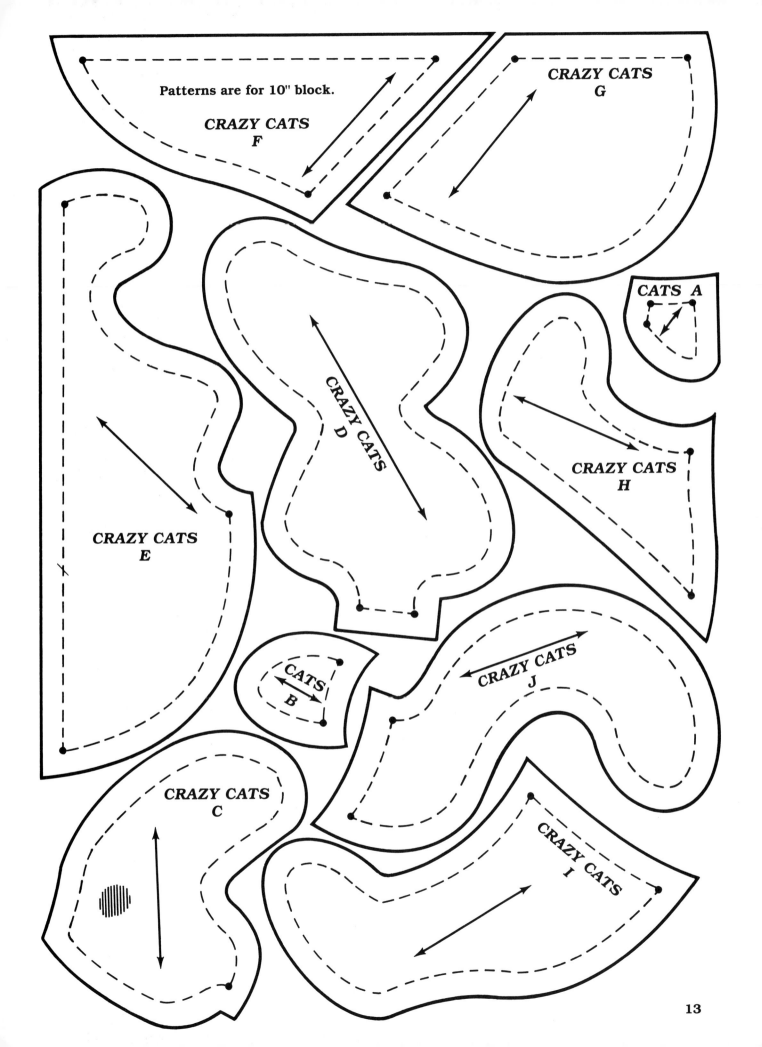

Patterns are for 10" block.

CRAZY CATS
F

CRAZY CATS
G

CATS A

CRAZY CATS
D

CRAZY CATS
H

CRAZY CATS
E

CATS
B

CRAZY CATS
J

CRAZY CATS
C

CRAZY CATS
I

13

Double Attic Windows

Many Attic Windows patterns have a single "frame" around the square window pieces. This Double Attic Windows features a two-tiered "frame" effect, which doubles your chances to play with this pattern's optical effects. Work it in light, medium, and dark tones of a single color or mix a number of colors, as you choose.

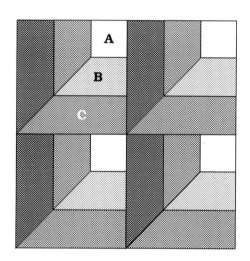

Block

FINISHED SIZE:
12" square

TYPE:
Four-patch

TEMPLATES:
3 (A-C)

PIECES PER BLOCK:
20

Square A:	4 white
Shape B:	4 light gray
B(rev):	4 medium gray
Shape C:	4 medium gray
C(rev):	4 dark gray

BLOCK ASSEMBLY:

To make a single quarter-unit: Join 1 B to 1 C; join B(r) to C(r). Join B/C and B(r)/C(r) units together along diagonal edge. Set in A. Repeat 3 times to make 4 quarter-units.

Join 2 quarter-units to make top half of block; repeat for bottom half. Join top and bottom halves of block.

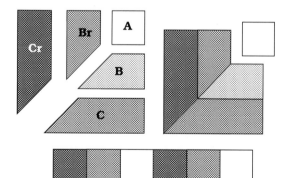

Large patterns are for 12" block. Small, gray
patterns are for 6" block.

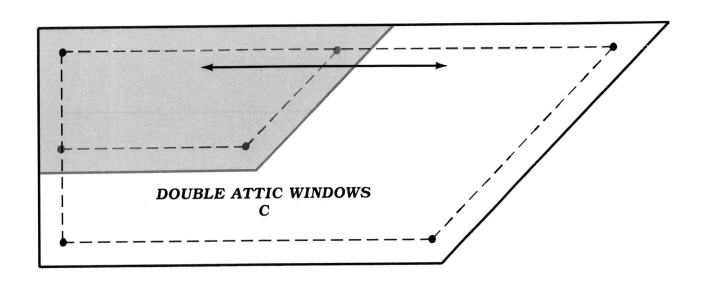

DOUBLE ATTIC WINDOWS
C

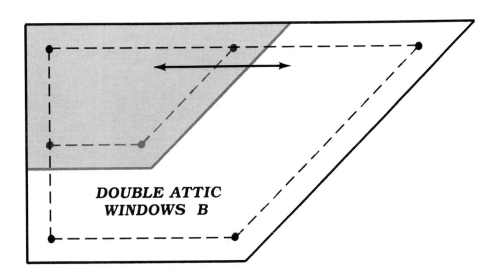

**DOUBLE ATTIC
WINDOWS B**

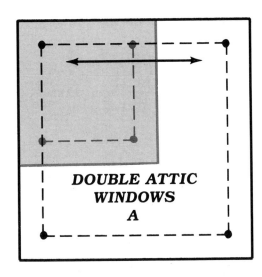

**DOUBLE ATTIC
WINDOWS
A**

Eight-Pointed Star

2 *The Eight-Pointed Star (sometimes called the LeMoyne Star when worked in alternating lights and darks) makes a twinkling addition to your collection of classic quilt patterns. For extra sparkle, try setting the blocks on point in a field of midnight blue.*

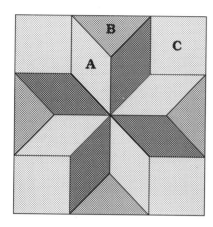

Block

FINISHED SIZE:
12" square

TYPE:
Diamonds

TEMPLATES:
3 (A-C)

PIECES PER BLOCK:
16

Diamond A: 4 light gray
 4 dark gray
Triangle B: 4 medium gray
Square C: 4 light gray

BLOCK ASSEMBLY:

To make the star, join diamond As into pairs. In circled areas, stitch only to seam allowance, stop, and backstitch to lock stitches in place. Trim away dog ears. Join the pairs together to make 2 sets of 4 diamonds (half-stars). Press the seam allowances in the 2 half-stars in opposite directions.

To complete star, join half-stars together, again stitching only to seam allowances in circled areas. On the wrong side of the block, at the center point of the star, remove stitching in the previous seams. This will allow the seam allowances of the diamonds to swirl around the center point of the star in a clockwise or counterclockwise manner. (See diagram at left.)

To finish block, set in 4 Bs, aligning 45-degree angles. Trim away dog ears. Then set in 4 Cs.

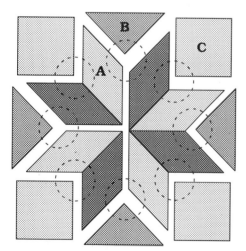

Large patterns are for 12" block. Small, gray patterns are for 6" block.

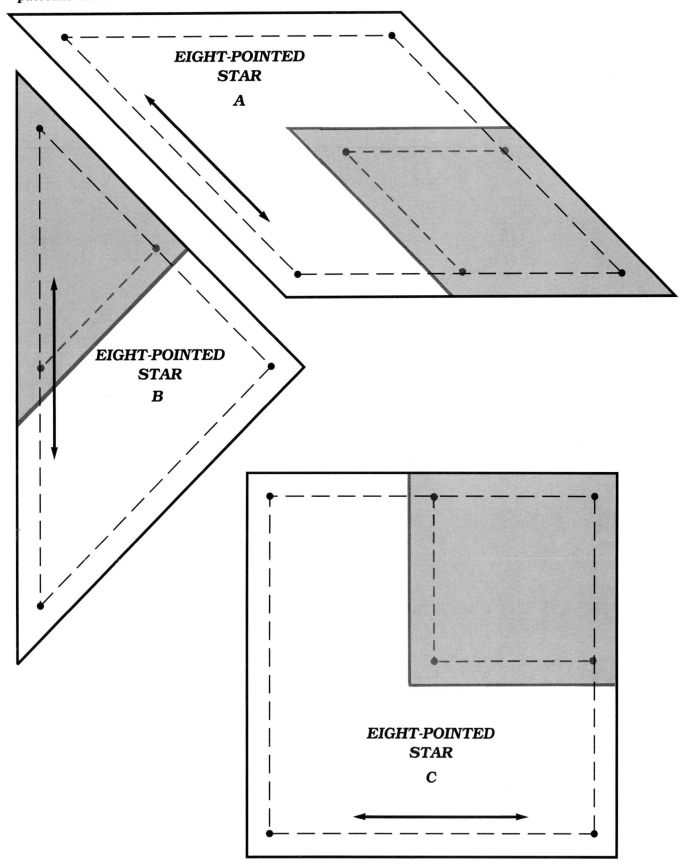

EIGHT-POINTED STAR A

EIGHT-POINTED STAR B

EIGHT-POINTED STAR C

Fancy Dresden Plate

This pattern is a scrap saver's dream, often done in pretty pastel prints that were lovingly gathered from the scrap basket. Try using a collection of clear, bright solids instead to give this old favorite a lively new look.

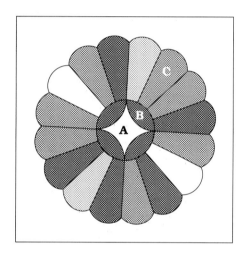

Block

FINISHED SIZE:
16" square

TYPE:
Circle in square

TEMPLATES:
3 (A-C)

PIECES PER BLOCK:
21 plus foundation block

Shape A: 1 white
Shape B: 4 dark gray
Shape C: 16 (various)

BLOCK ASSEMBLY:
   Piece 4 Bs to A to form center circle. Join all Cs into pairs, then into 4 groups of 4 Cs, then into 2 groups of 8 Cs, and then into a ring of 16 Cs. Turn under inner circle seam allowance of C-ring; appliqué ring to center circle. Appliqué completed plate to 16" (add seam allowances) foundation block.
   Alternate method: Join 4 Cs together; piece to a single B. Repeat 3 more times. Piece 4 B/C units to A, first completing A/B seams and then stitching C/C seams. Appliqué plate to foundation block.

Large patterns are for 16" block. Small, gray
patterns are for 6" block.

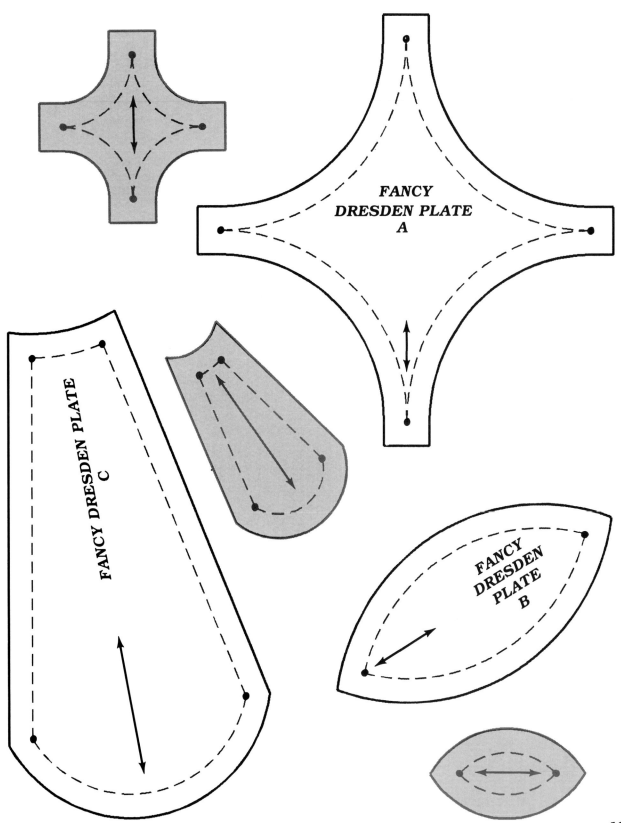

FANCY
DRESDEN PLATE
A

FANCY DRESDEN PLATE
C

FANCY
DRESDEN
PLATE
B

19

Flying Dutchman

2   *According to an old sea story, the Flying Dutchman is a phantom ship sometimes seen in the stormy winds off the Cape of Good Hope. Its captain, so the story goes, was guilty of an oath so dreadful that, for punishment, he was doomed to sail the lonely, storm-tossed seas forever.*

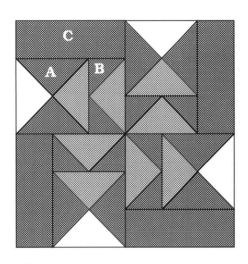

Block

FINISHED SIZE:
12" square

TYPE:
Four-patch

TEMPLATES:
3 (A-C)

PIECES PER BLOCK:
32

Triangle A: 4 white
                  8 medium gray
                  8 dark gray
Triangle B: 8 dark gray
Rectangle C: 4 dark gray

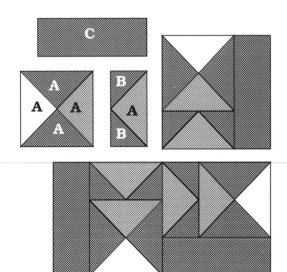

BLOCK ASSEMBLY:
   Join 4 triangles A (1 white, 1 medium gray, and 2 dark gray) together to make a square. Join 2 dark gray Bs to medium gray A to make a rectangle. Join A/A/A/A square and B/A/B rectangle. Join rectangle C along top edge of pieced unit to complete quarter-block. Repeat 3 times for 4 quarter-blocks.
   Join 2 quarter-blocks to make half-block. Repeat. Join half-blocks.

Large patterns are for 12" block. Small, gray
patterns are for 6" block.

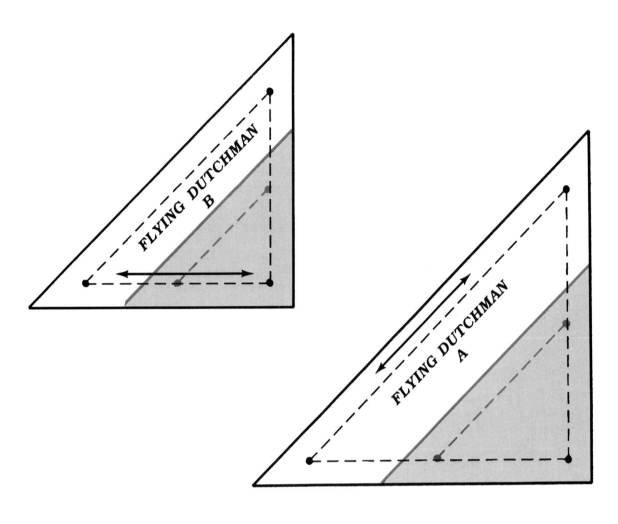

FLYING DUTCHMAN
B

FLYING DUTCHMAN
A

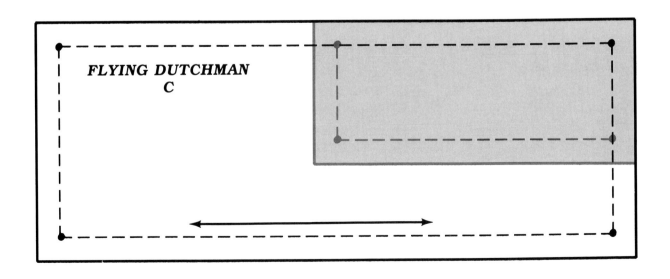

FLYING DUTCHMAN
C

Flying Swallows

3   *Spinning Spools member Irene Dulaney, of Belle Rive, Illinois, sent a photo of a striking quilt made years ago by her mother, Caroline Catron. Its traditional pattern, Flying Swallows, offers a wonderful sense of energy and movement, no matter what colors are used to piece it. But the red, yellow, and white combination used in Irene's quilt really makes these Flying Swallows sing!*

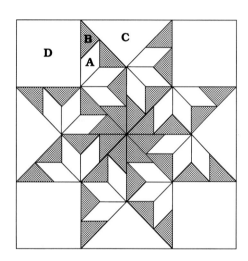

Block

FINISHED SIZE:
18" square

TYPE:
Diamonds

TEMPLATES:
4 (A-D)

PIECES PER BLOCK:
64

Diamond A:	24 white
Triangle B:	32 medium gray
Triangle C:	4 white
Square D:	4 white

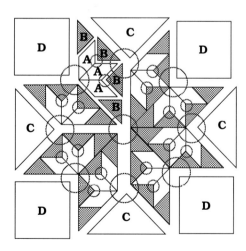

BLOCK ASSEMBLY:

Note: When setting in right-angled pieces or joining diamonds into a star, remember to stitch only to the seam allowance line, stop, and backstitch. Circled areas on the piecing diagram show piecing situations in which this is important. The small turning dots on your templates can be very helpful here. Punch out the turning dots with a ⅛" hole punch and mark the turning dot with a pencil on your cloth pattern piece. The dot will remind you not to sew into the seam allowance.

To make each large diamond unit of star, join 3 As together. Add 4 Bs, setting into As as shown.

Make 8 large diamond units. Join together, one at a time, sewing just to seam allowance and backstitching at center point, to leave free-floating seam allowances that twirl around center point.

Set in 4 Cs as shown. Set in 4 Ds.

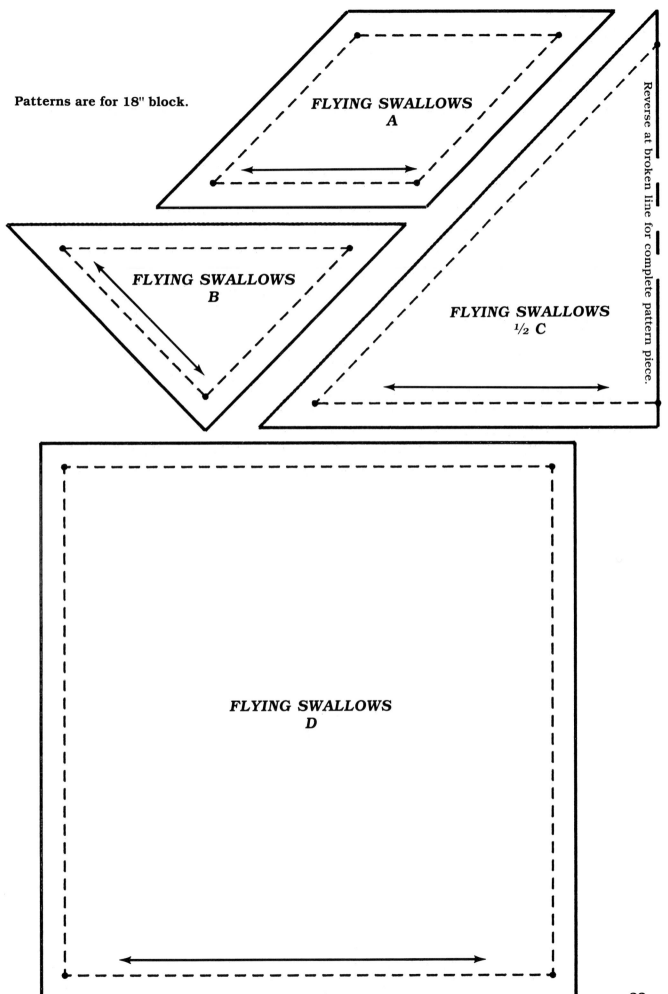

Patterns are for 18" block.

FLYING SWALLOWS
A

FLYING SWALLOWS
B

FLYING SWALLOWS
½ C

Reverse at broken line for complete pattern piece.

FLYING SWALLOWS
D

Indian Meadows

2 *Many Spinning Spools members enjoy using quilt patterns showing Native American influence. Indian Meadows is one of a series of patterns from Spinning Spools—including both traditional and original designs—that reflect the Native American way of life.*

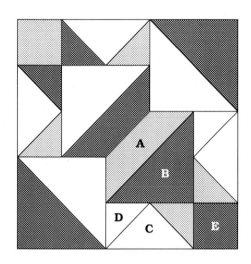

Block

FINISHED SIZE:
12" square

TYPE:
Miscellaneous

TEMPLATES:
5 (A-E)

PIECES PER BLOCK:
22

Trapezoid A:	1 light gray
	1 dark gray
Triangle B:	3 dark gray
	3 white
Triangle C:	4 white
Triangle D:	2 dark gray
	4 light gray
	2 white
Square E:	1 light gray
	1 dark gray

BLOCK ASSEMBLY:

To make Unit 1, join 1 dark gray B to 1 white triangle B. Repeat for a second B/B Unit 1.

Make Unit 2: Join 1 light gray A to 1 dark gray B. Join 1 white C to 1 white D and 1 light gray D. Repeat for a second D/C/D unit. Join A/B unit to 1 D/C/D unit. Join second D/C/D unit to dark gray square E. Join A/B/D/C/D to D/C/D/E to complete Unit 2. Repeat with remaining pieces for a second Unit 2.

Join 2 Units 2 as shown. Set in 2 Units 1 to complete block.

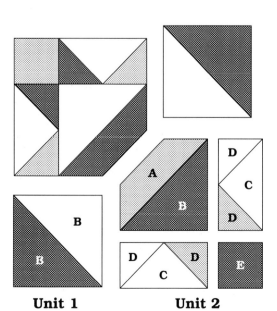

Unit 1   **Unit 2**

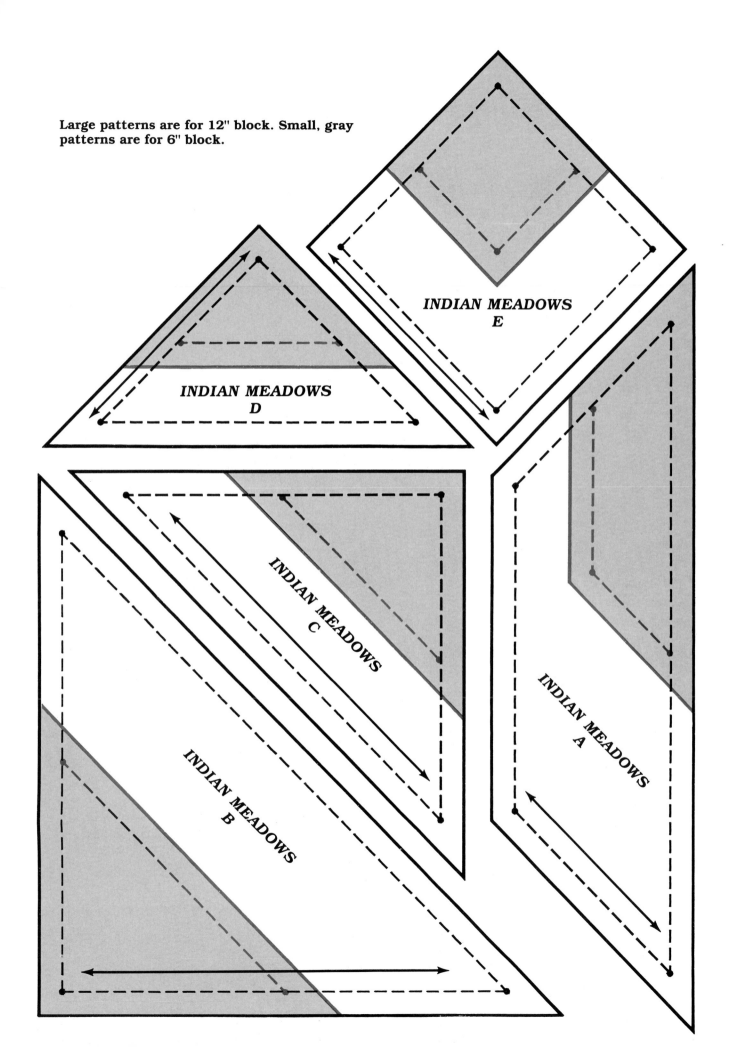

Large patterns are for 12" block. Small, gray patterns are for 6" block.

INDIAN MEADOWS
E

INDIAN MEADOWS
D

INDIAN MEADOWS
C

INDIAN MEADOWS
B

INDIAN MEADOWS
A

Joseph's Coat

2   Many Spinning Spools members collect quilt patterns with a biblical theme, and so we have included a number of biblical patterns in the Spinning Spools collection. This block, for example, Joseph's Coat, is one of a group of Spinning Spools patterns taken from a biblical sampler quilt which Georgia made early in her career.

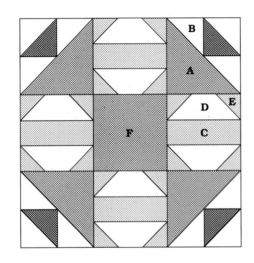

Block

FINISHED SIZE:
12" square

TYPE:
Nine-patch

TEMPLATES:
6 (A-F)

PIECES PER BLOCK:
49

Triangle A:	4 medium gray
Triangle B:	4 dark gray
	12 white
Rectangle C:	4 light gray
Trapezoid D:	8 white
Triangle E:	16 light gray
Square F:	1 medium gray

BLOCK ASSEMBLY:

To make Unit 1, use 1 A, 3 white Bs, and 1 dark gray B. Piece together as shown in piecing option 1 or 2. Repeat for a total of 4 Units 1. To make Unit 2, use 1 C, 2 Ds, and 4 Es. Repeat to make a total of 4 Units 2.

Arrange Units 1 and 2 with 1 square F in 3 rows of 3 squares each, as shown. Join units in each horizontal row. Join rows to complete block.

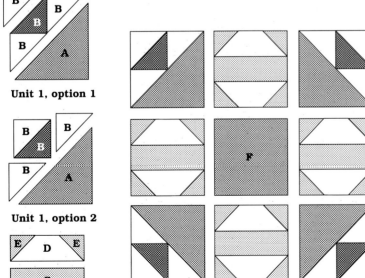

Unit 1, option 1

Unit 1, option 2

Unit 2

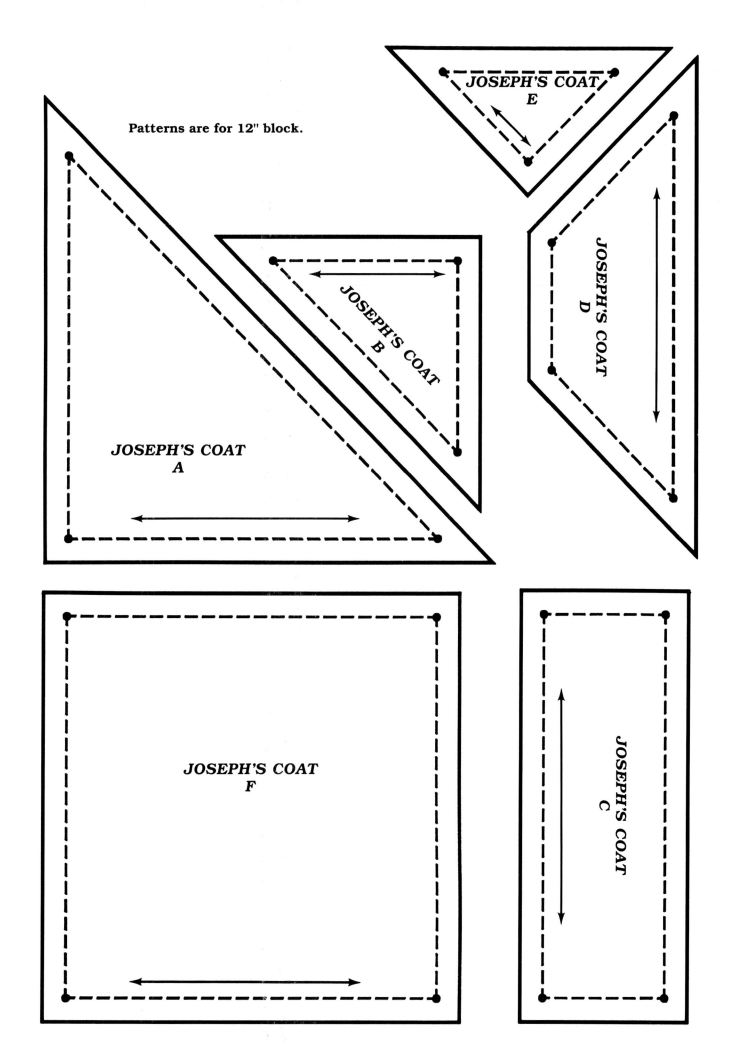

Patterns are for 12" block.

JOSEPH'S COAT
E

JOSEPH'S COAT
B

JOSEPH'S COAT
D

JOSEPH'S COAT
A

JOSEPH'S COAT
F

JOSEPH'S COAT
C

Missouri Star

 Missouri is the "show me" state, and with the traditional Missouri Star, we'll show you a wonderfully sparkling design.

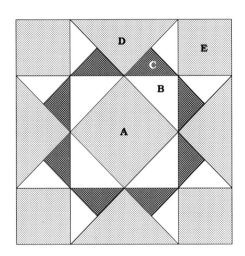

Block

FINISHED SIZE:
12" square

TYPE:
Nine-patch

TEMPLATES:
5 (A-E)

PIECES PER BLOCK:
29

Square A:	1 light gray
Triangle B:	4 white
Triangle C:	8 dark gray
	8 white
Triangle D:	4 light gray
Square E:	4 light gray

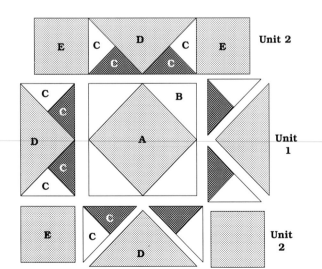

BLOCK ASSEMBLY:

 To make Unit 1, join 2 dark gray Cs to 2 white Cs. Join C/C and C/C to 1 D. Repeat for a second C/C/D/C/C section. Join 4 Bs to A. Join C/C/D/C/C section, B/B/B/B/A section, and second C/C/D/C/C section to complete Unit 1.

 For Unit 2, first join 2 dark gray Cs to 2 white Cs. Then join E, C/C, D, C/C, E to make Unit 2. Repeat for a second Unit 2. Join Unit 1 and 2 Units 2.

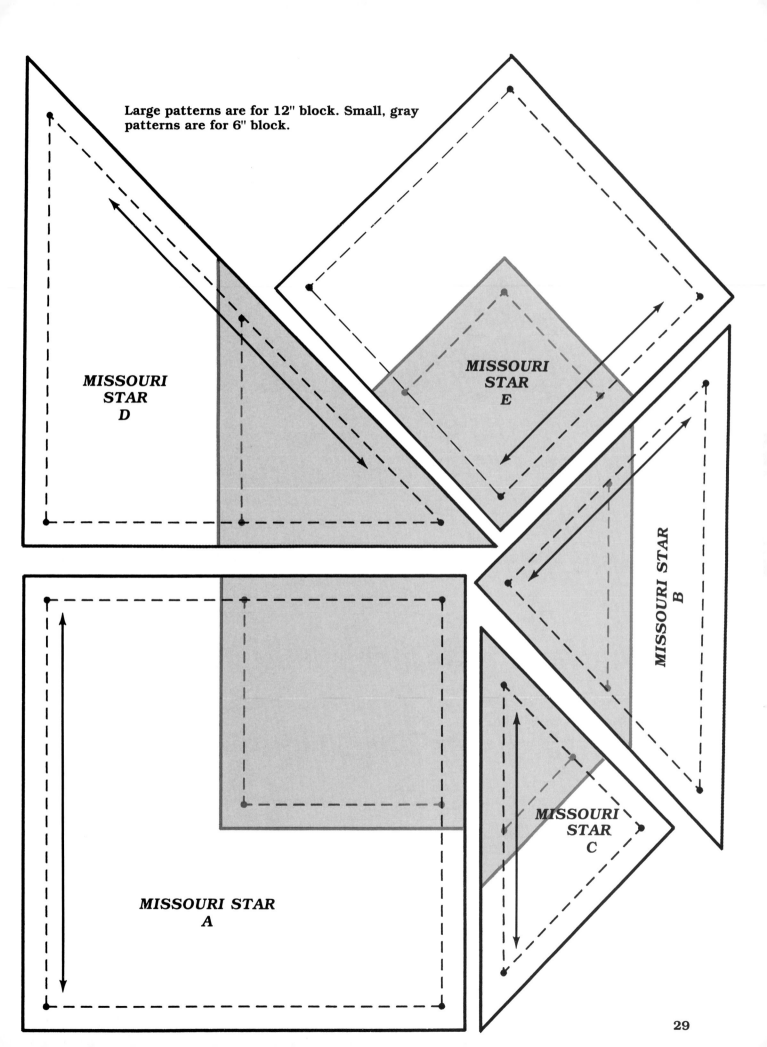

Large patterns are for 12" block. Small, gray
patterns are for 6" block.

MISSOURI
STAR
D

MISSOURI
STAR
E

MISSOURI STAR
B

MISSOURI
STAR
C

MISSOURI STAR
A

Mother's Dream

2 *What do you suppose Mother was dreaming of? Piece this old traditional pattern in a variety of rich, clear solids and you will achieve the effect of stained glass windows or a box of sparkling jewels.*

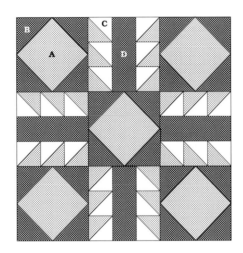

Block

FINISHED SIZE:
15" square

TYPE:
Nine-patch

TEMPLATES:
4 (A-D)

PIECES PER BLOCK:
77

Square A:	5 light gray
Triangle B:	20 dark gray
Triangle C:	24 white
	24 light gray
Rectangle D:	4 dark gray

BLOCK ASSEMBLY:

To make Unit 1 (diamond in square unit), join 4 Bs to 1 A. Repeat 4 times, to make a total of 5 diamond-in-square units.

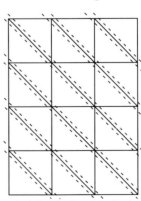

Quick Piecing Method

To make Unit 2 squares (feathered squares): Join 24 light gray Cs to 24 white Cs. (*For quick piecing*: Place light gray and white fabric right sides together. On wrong side of white fabric, trace around C template 24 times, as shown in diagram. Stitch ¼" seams on each side of diagonal lines. Cut triangles apart and press open for 24 C/C light gray/white squares.)

Join C/C squares in strips of 3, as shown. Join 2 feathered strips with 1 D to make feathered Unit 2. Repeat for a total of 4.

Alternate Units 1 and 2 in 3 rows of 3 as shown and join.

Unit 1   Unit 2

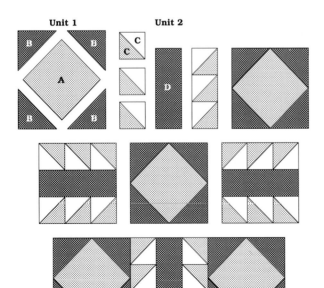

Large patterns are for 15" block. Small, gray
patterns are for 6" block.

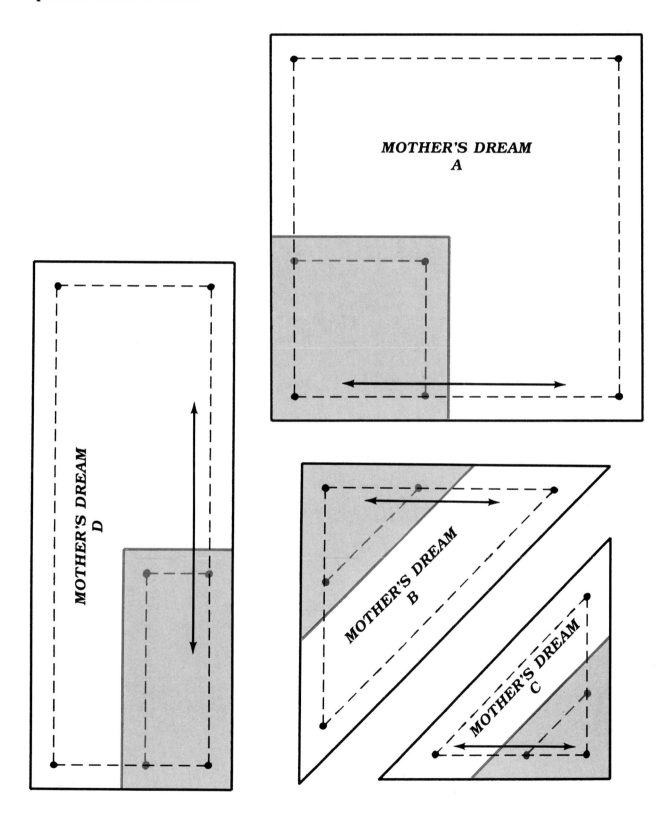

MOTHER'S DREAM
A

MOTHER'S DREAM
D

MOTHER'S DREAM
B

MOTHER'S DREAM
C

Oak Leaf & Reel

2️⃣ *Here's a classic appliqué pattern that was loved by our pioneer grandmothers. The Oak Leaf & Reel pattern illustrated here is taken from a quilt in the collection of the Tennessee State Museum in Nashville, Tennessee.*

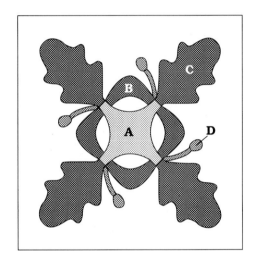

Block

FINISHED SIZE:
16" square

TYPE:
Appliqué

TEMPLATES:
4 (A-D)

PIECES PER BLOCK:
17 plus foundation block

Shape A:	1 light gray
Shape B:	4 dark gray
Shape C:	4 dark gray
Shape D:	4 medium gray
Bias Stems:	4 medium gray

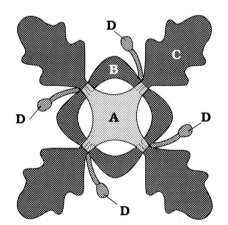

BLOCK ASSEMBLY:

Mark 16" (add seam allowances) foundation block for placement of appliqué.

Appliqué 4 Bs, 4 Ds, and bias-strip stems in place. Then appliqué 4 Cs and A in place, covering edges of earlier appliqué.

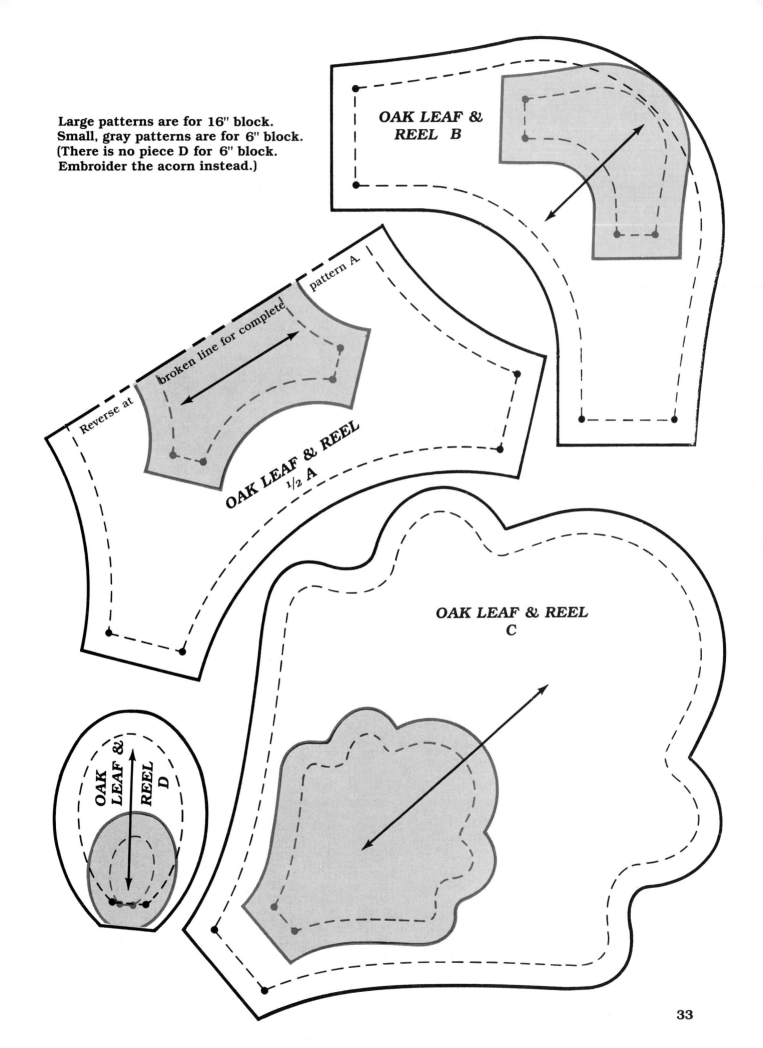

Large patterns are for 16" block.
Small, gray patterns are for 6" block.
(There is no piece D for 6" block.
Embroider the acorn instead.)

OAK LEAF &
REEL B

Reverse at broken line for complete pattern A.

OAK LEAF & REEL
½ A

OAK LEAF & REEL
C

OAK
LEAF &
REEL
D

Old Maid's Puzzle

2 *Spinning Spools member Janet Adams of McMinnville, Oregon, wrote with an interesting idea. She sent a photograph of a sampler quilt top she had made and stretched on a wooden frame lined with corkboard, to serve as a decorative wall hanging and a pull-down cutting board. One of the blocks Janet used in her sampler was the traditional Old Maid's Puzzle.*

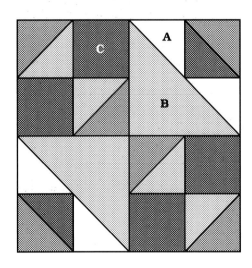

Block

FINISHED SIZE:
12" square

TYPE:
Four-patch

TEMPLATES:
3 (A-C)

PIECES PER BLOCK:
22

Triangle A:	4 light gray
	4 white
	6 medium gray
	2 dark gray
Triangle B:	2 medium gray
Square C:	4 dark gray

Unit 1

Unit 2

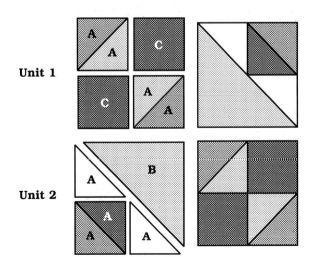

BLOCK ASSEMBLY:

Join 1 light gray A to 1 medium gray A. Repeat for second A/A square. To each A/A square, join a dark gray square C as shown. Join the 2 A/A/C units together to make Unit 1. Repeat for second Unit 1.

To make Unit 2, join medium gray A to dark gray A. Join 2 white As to A/A square just made. Join B. Repeat for second Unit 2.

Join 1 Unit 1 to 1 Unit 2 for left half of block. Repeat, reversing positions, for right half of block. Join left and right halves of block.

Large patterns are for 12" block. Small, gray patterns are for 6" block.

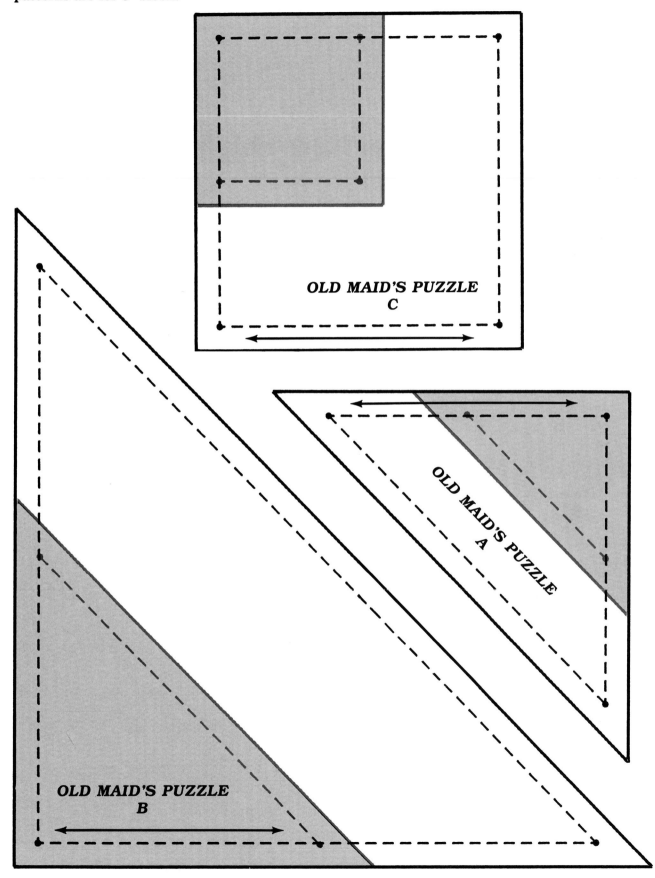

OLD MAID'S PUZZLE
C

OLD MAID'S PUZZLE
A

OLD MAID'S PUZZLE
B

Old-Fashioned Nosegay

Grandma's favorites included all the dear, old-fashioned scrap-bag patterns, like the nosegay design that we show here. She pieced these blocks from soft florals, other delicate prints, and scraps of solids. And the bouquets that resulted were as sweet as a gathering of flowers from her summer garden: roses, asters, amaranth, and columbine.

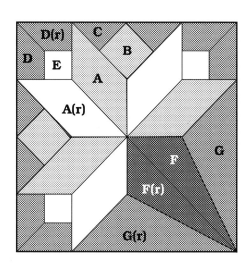

Block

FINISHED SIZE:
14" square

TYPE:
Miscellaneous

TEMPLATES:
7 (A-G)

PIECES PER BLOCK:
25

Parallelogram A:	3 light gray
A(rev):	3 white
Square B:	2 light gray
Triangle C:	4 medium gray
Shape D:	3 medium gray
D(rev):	3 medium gray
Square E:	3 white
Triangle F:	1 dark gray
F(rev):	1 dark gray
Triangle G:	1 medium gray
G(rev):	1 medium gray

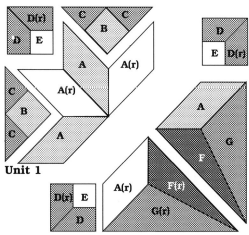

Unit 1

Unit 2

BLOCK ASSEMBLY:

Join 1 B to 2 Cs. Repeat for a total of 2 C/B/C units. Join D to E. Set in D(rev) for D/E/D(rev) unit. Join A to A(rev); repeat, and join 2 A/A(rev) units together to make A/A(rev)/A/A(rev) unit. Sct 2 C/B/C units and D/E/D(rcv) unit into A/A(rev)/A/A(rev) unit to make Unit 1.

For Unit 2, make 2 more D/E/D(rev) units. Join 1 F to 1 G and set in A for A/F/G unit. Repeat, using reversed shapes, for A(rev)/F(rev)/G(rev) unit. Join D/E/D(rev) unit, A(rev)/F(rev)/G(rev) unit, A/F/G unit, and D/E/D(rev) unit as shown to make Unit 2.

Join Unit 1 to Unit 2 to complete block.

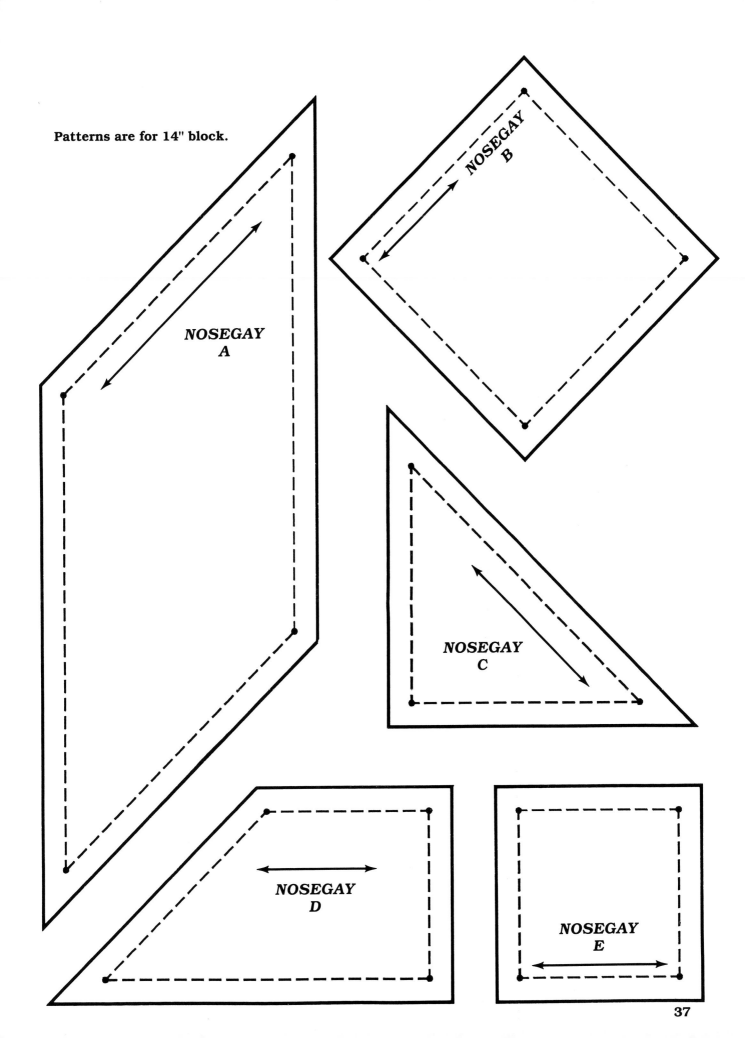

Patterns are for 14" block.

NOSEGAY
A

NOSEGAY
B

NOSEGAY
C

NOSEGAY
D

NOSEGAY
E

37

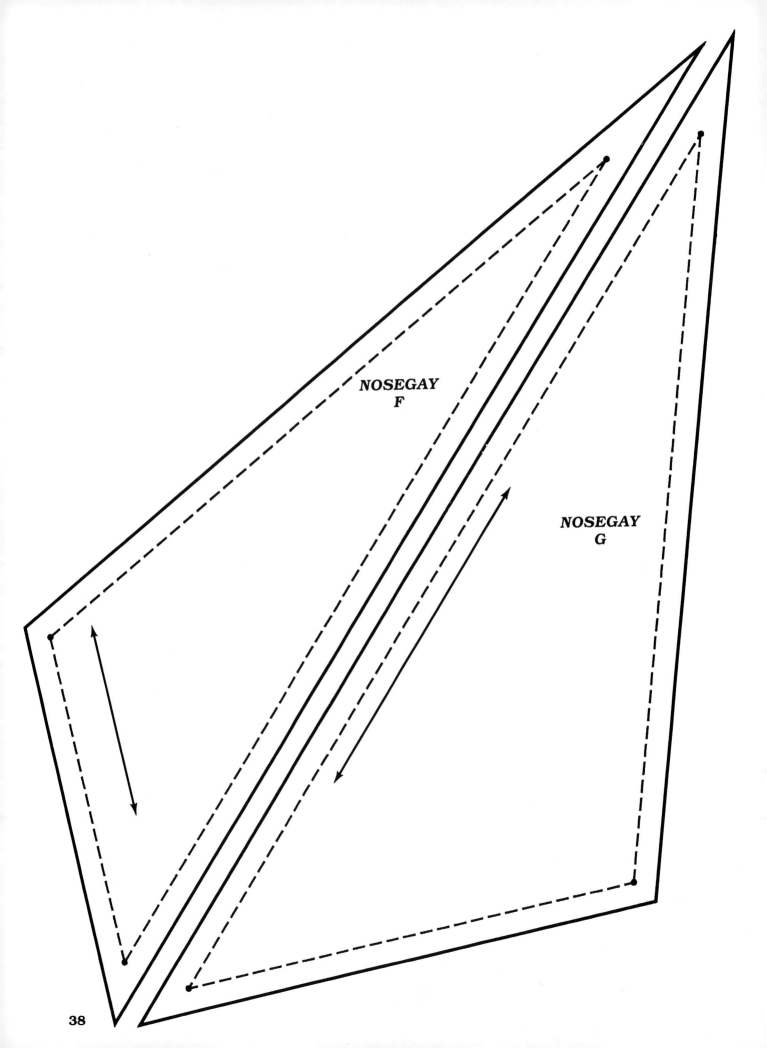

NOSEGAY
F

NOSEGAY
G

38

Pinwheel

Pinwheel is a playful pattern with lots of movement and energy. Make it in bright, bold colors perfect for the playroom. It doesn't take advanced skills to set this pretty pattern in motion—even beginners will enjoy the Pinwheel block.

Block

FINISHED SIZE:
12" square

TYPE:
Four-patch

TEMPLATES:
2 (A-B)

PIECES PER BLOCK:
16

Triangle A: 4 dark gray
4 light gray
4 white

Shape B: 4 white

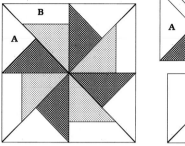
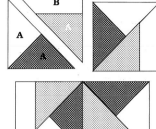

BLOCK ASSEMBLY:

Join 1 light gray A to 1 white B; join 1 dark gray A to 1 white A. Join A/B unit to A/A unit to make a quarter-block. Repeat 3 times for a total of 4 quarter-blocks.

Join 2 quarter-blocks together to make a half-block. Repeat. Join 2 half-blocks.

Large patterns are for 12" block.
Small, gray patterns are
for 6" block.

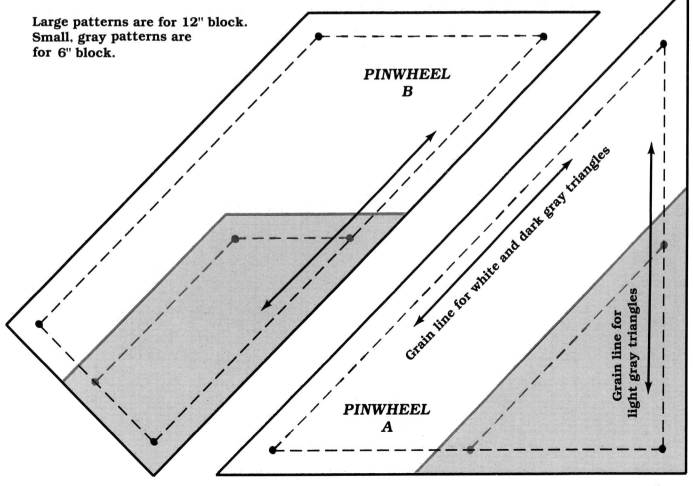

PINWHEEL
B

PINWHEEL
A

Grain line for white and dark gray triangles

Grain line for
light gray triangles

Shaded Trail

Spinning Spools member Moneisa Magnuson of East Helena, Montana, was born in Kansas. When she moved to Montana as a child, she had never seen pine trees or mountains and still recalls the awe she felt at first encountering Montana's green mountains. To celebrate Montana's centennial year, Moneisa stitched a wall hanging based on the traditional block Shaded Trail.

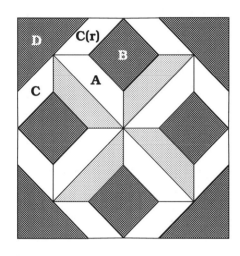

Block

FINISHED SIZE:
12" square

TYPE:
Miscellaneous

TEMPLATES:
4 (A-D)

PIECES PER BLOCK:
24

Trapezoid A:	4 white
	4 light gray
Square B:	4 dark gray
Parallelogram C:	4 white
C(rev):	4 white
Triangle D:	4 dark gray

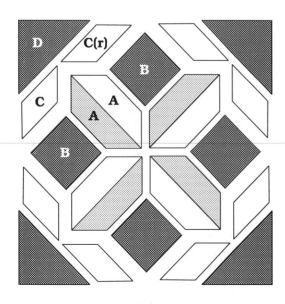

BLOCK ASSEMBLY:
Join 1 white A to 1 light gray A; repeat for 4 A/A shapes. Join A/A shapes together one at a time, stitching only to center seam allowance to leave free-floating seam allowances that twirl around center point. Set in 4 Bs. Set in Cs and Cs(rev). Set in Ds.

Large patterns are for 12" block. Small, gray patterns are for 6" block.

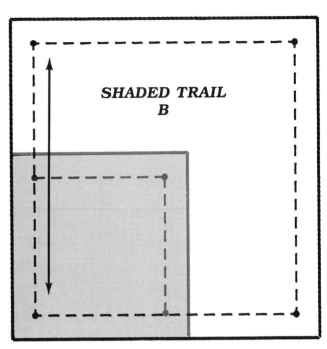

SHADED TRAIL
B

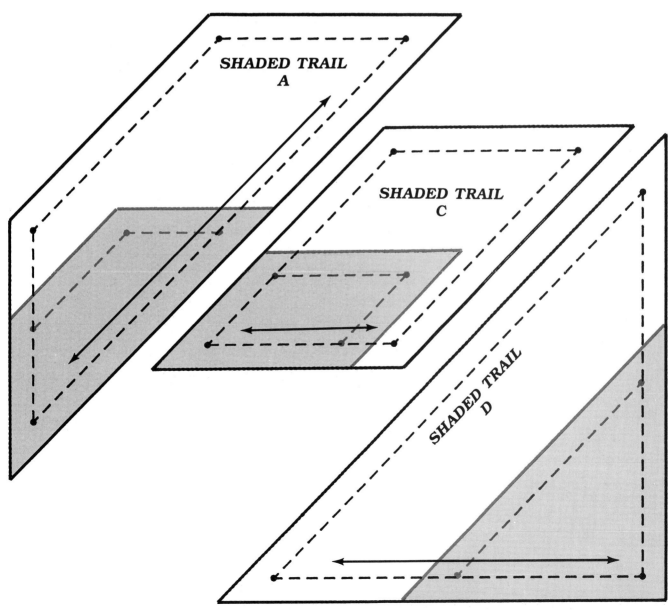

SHADED TRAIL
A

SHADED TRAIL
C

SHADED TRAIL
D

Star of Bethlehem

Here is another block from Georgia's biblical sampler. The Star of Bethlehem block offers a combination of piecing and appliqué for those of you who enjoy both techniques. Using a print for piece B adds interest to the star.

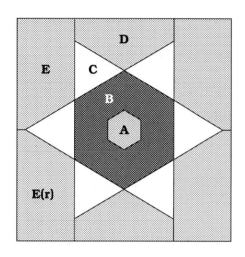

Block

FINISHED SIZE:
12" square

TYPE:
Star

TEMPLATES:
5 (A-E)

PIECES PER BLOCK:
14

Hexagon A:	1 light gray
Hexagon B:	1 dark gray
Triangle C:	6 white
Shape D:	2 light gray
Shape E:	2 light gray
E(rev):	2 light gray

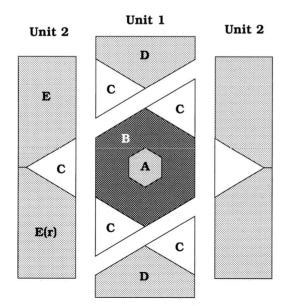

BLOCK ASSEMBLY:
　　To make Unit 1, appliqué A to B. Join 2 Cs to A/B. Join 1 C to 1 D. Repeat. Join C/Ds to C/A/B/C.
　　To make Unit 2, join 1 E and 1 E(rev) to 1 C. Repeat for a second Unit 2. Join 2 Units 2 to Unit 1 to complete block.

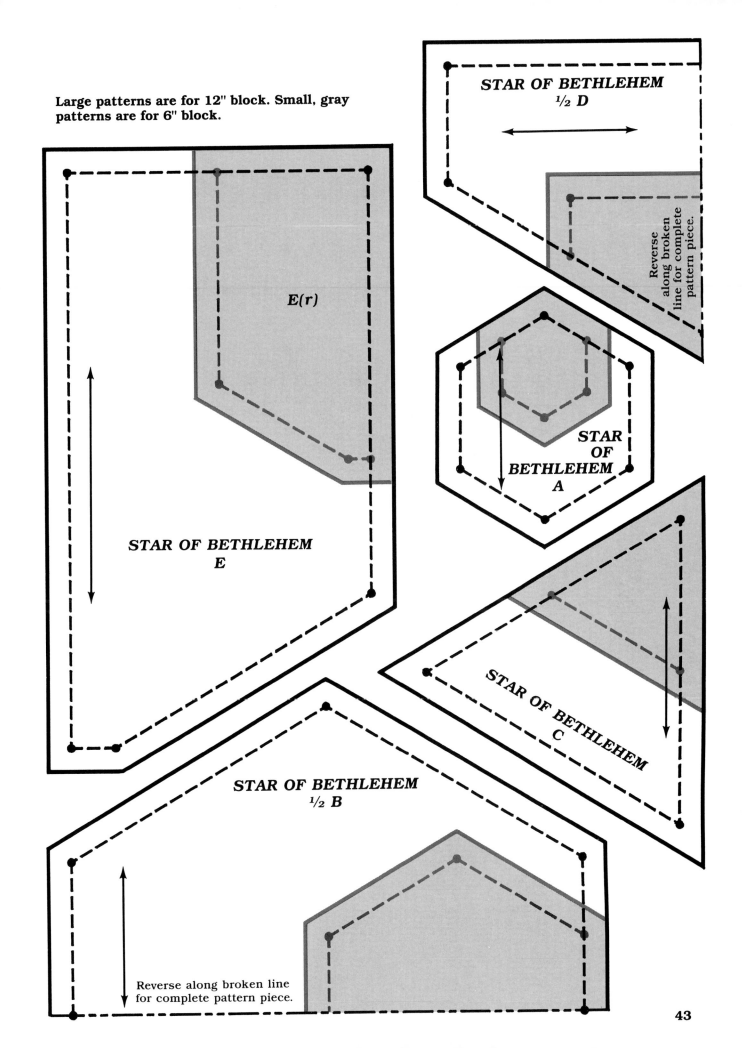

Large patterns are for 12" block. Small, gray patterns are for 6" block.

STAR OF BETHLEHEM
½ D

Reverse along broken line for complete pattern piece.

E(r)

STAR OF BETHLEHEM
E

STAR
OF
BETHLEHEM
A

STAR OF BETHLEHEM
C

STAR OF BETHLEHEM
½ B

Reverse along broken line for complete pattern piece.

Tall Pine Tree

1 *With a block-to-block setting and some imaginative use of color, the traditional pattern Tall Pine Tree can become a fabric painting of pine trees in the mountains. Choose a variety of purple, blue, green, and brown fabrics. Use predominantly darker tones near the base of the work and add lighter tones as you move toward the top of the piece, so that the pine trees seem to rise up into cool, fresh mountain air.*

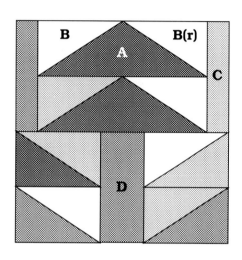

Block

FINISHED SIZE:
12" square

TYPE:
Picture block

TEMPLATES:
4 (A–D)

PIECES PER BLOCK:
17

Triangle A:	2 dark gray
Triangle B:	2 white
	3 light gray
	1 medium gray
B(rev):	3 white
	1 light gray
	1 medium gray
	1 dark gray
Rectangle C:	1 light gray
	1 medium gray
Rectangle D:	1 medium gray

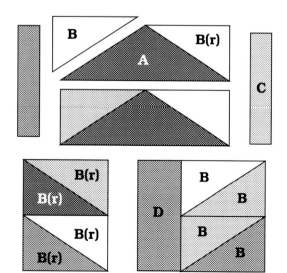

BLOCK ASSEMBLY:

Join 1 A and 1 B; add 1 B(r) to complete rectangle. Repeat for second B/A/B(r) rectangle. Join 2 rectangles together. Join C strips on 2 ends of large pieced rectangle as shown, to complete upper half of block.

Join 2 Bs to 2 more Bs as shown. Join the 2 B/B units together to make lower right unit of block; repeat with 4 B(r) shapes for lower left unit. Join both units with D strip for lower half of block. Join upper and lower halves of blocks.

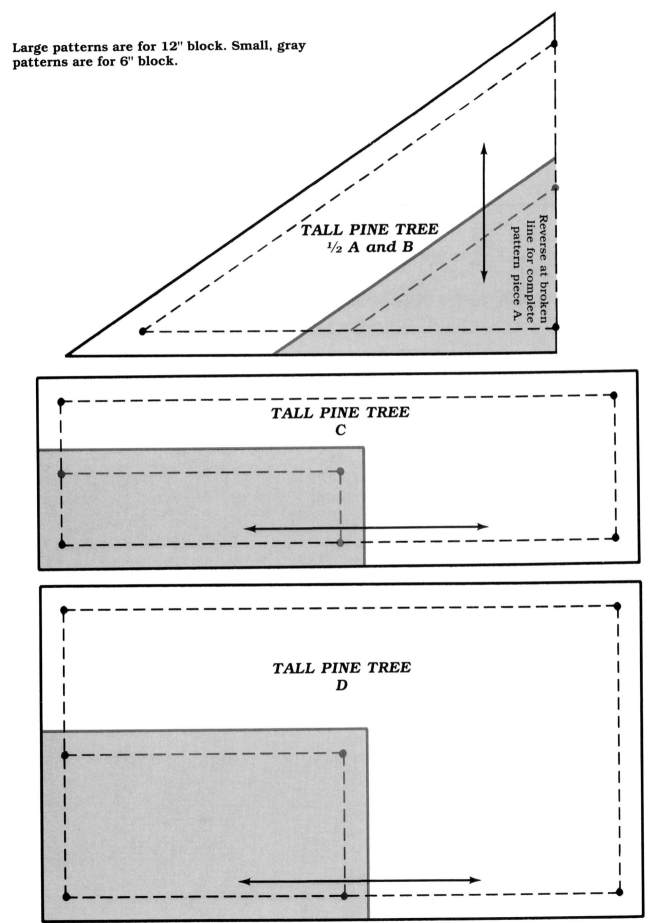

Large patterns are for 12" block. Small, gray patterns are for 6" block.

TALL PINE TREE
½ A and B

Reverse at broken line for complete pattern piece A.

TALL PINE TREE
C

TALL PINE TREE
D

Weathervane

2 *Growing up in the Adirondack Mountains, Spinning Spools member Louisa Wilson of Cadyville, New York, found great inspiration for the country designs she loves. Louisa likes to spice traditional patchwork with machine appliqué, as in her delightful Weathervane block.*

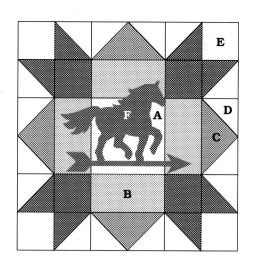

Block

FINISHED SIZE:
12" square

TYPE:
Gridded block with appliqué

TEMPLATES:
6 (A-F)

PIECES PER BLOCK:
42

Square A:	1 white
Rectangle B:	4 light gray
Triangle C:	4 medium gray
Triangle D:	16 white
	8 dark gray
Square E:	4 white
	4 dark gray
Shape F1:	1 dark gray
Shape F2:	1 dark gray

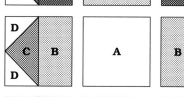 

BLOCK ASSEMBLY:
To piece block as a 9-patch, make 4 D/D/E/D/D/E squares and 4 D/C/D/B squares, as shown. Join with 1 A square to complete block. Appliqué F1 and F2 in place.

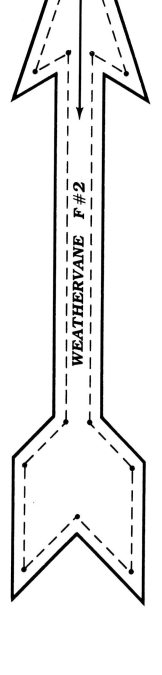

WEATHERVANE F #2

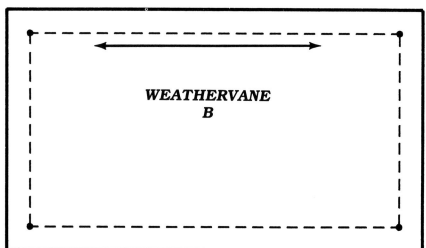

WEATHERVANE
B

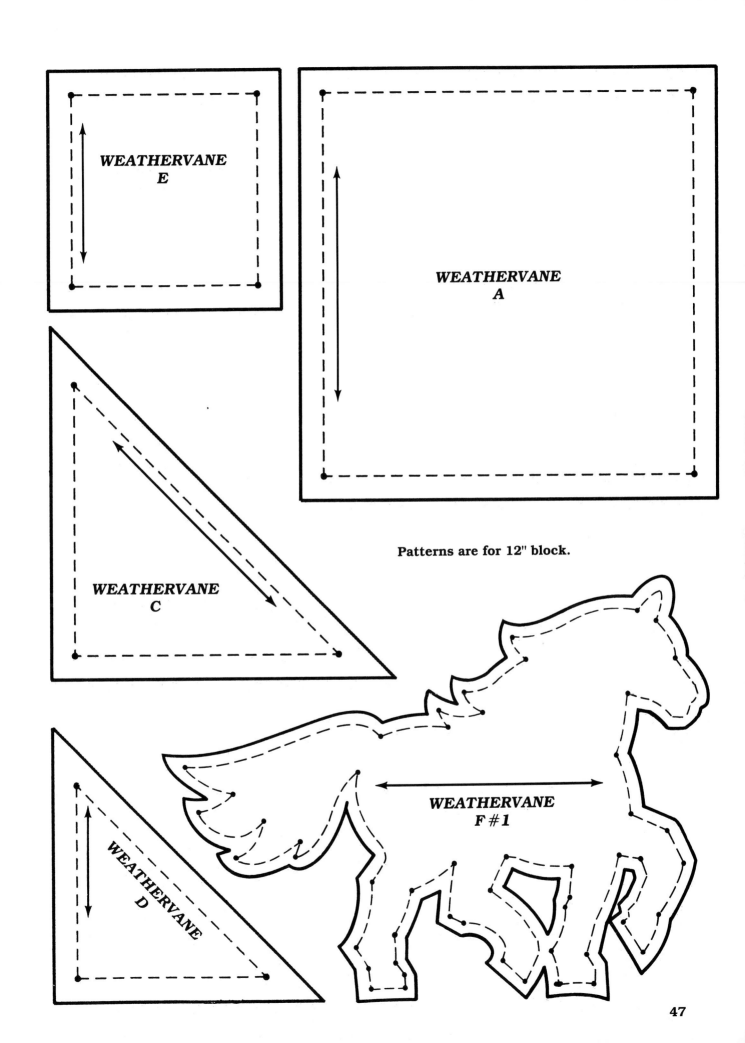

WEATHERVANE
E

WEATHERVANE
A

WEATHERVANE
C

Patterns are for 12" block.

WEATHERVANE
F #1

WEATHERVANE
D

Wheels

2 *Wheels is an intriguing old pattern that has kept generations of quilters going around in circles! The pattern we present here was taken from a handsome brown and gold antique Wheels quilt in the collection of the Tennessee State Museum.*

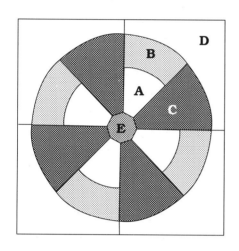

Block

FINISHED SIZE:
15" square

TYPE:
Circle in a square

TEMPLATES:
5 (A-E)

PIECES PER BLOCK:
17

Shape A:	4 white
Shape B:	4 light gray
Shape C:	4 dark gray
Shape D:	4 white
Octagon E:	1 medium gray

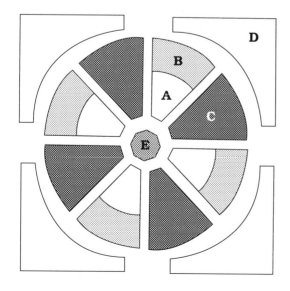

BLOCK ASSEMBLY:
Join 1 A to 1 B. Join A/B unit to C. Join A/B/C to D to complete 1 quarter unit of block (except for center). Repeat 3 more times for a total of 4 quarter units.

Join quarter units together. Set piece E into center of block.

Alternate method: Join A to B. Join A/B to C. Repeat for total of 4 A/B/C units. Join units together, and set piece E into center to complete wheel. Appliqué wheel onto center of 15½" square of background fabric.

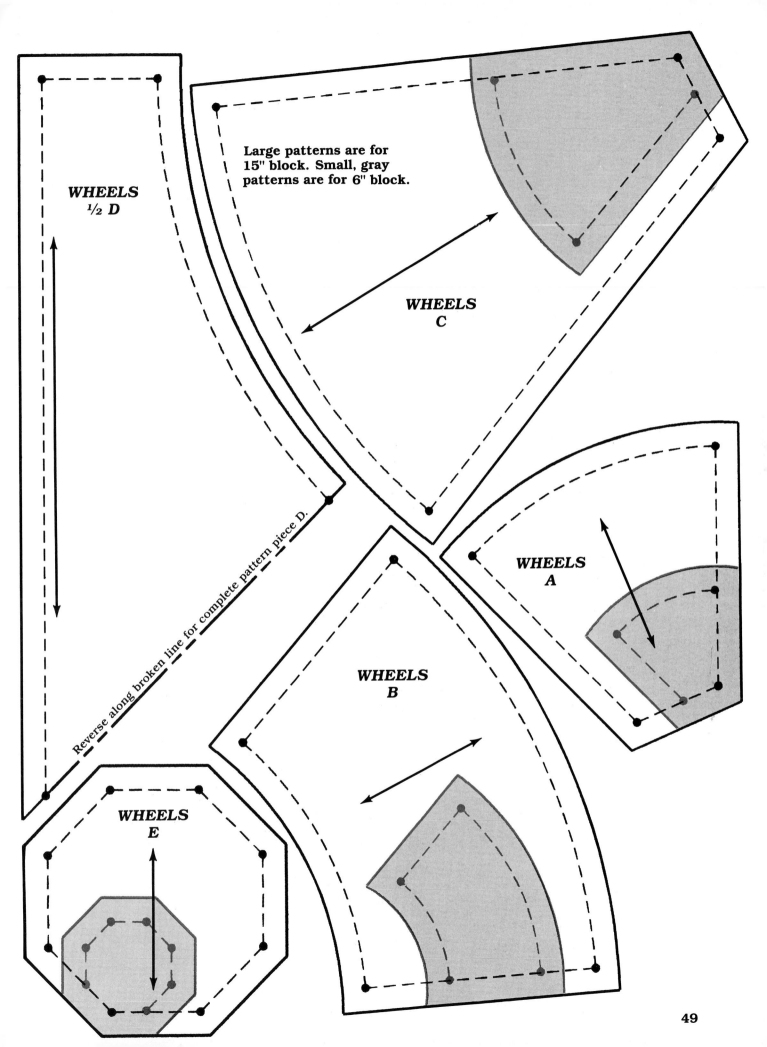

WHEELS
½ D

Large patterns are for
15" block. Small, gray
patterns are for 6" block.

WHEELS
C

Reverse along broken line for complete pattern piece D.

WHEELS
A

WHEELS
B

WHEELS
E

Spinning Spools Projects

The Spinning Spools Pattern Club
offers dozens of ideas for interesting projects
to make with quilt blocks—in addition
to quilts and wall hangings.
In Spinning Spools, there are instructions for
quilted tote bags, a table cover, table runners,
collars, a granny gown, sweatshirts, vests,
and many other items to fill your home
and to offer as welcome gifts.
In the following pages,
you'll find two examples of small
projects from Spinning Spools—a handy
Sweet-Gum Chair Pocket and an
attractive Fan Fire Screen.

Sweet-Gum Chair Pocket

1 *Do you have a chair for lap quilting—one that is cushy for hours, in good light, and most important, places you at the heart of your family's activities? Then make that favorite chair even more stitcher-friendly with an over-the-arm organizer to hold all your tools and supplies for the work at hand. This one hides those handy items in a pretty Sweet-Gum Leaf pocket.*

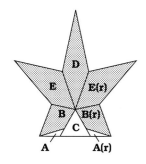

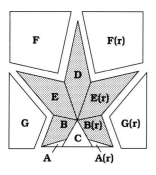

Block

FINISHED SIZE:
10" square

TYPE:
Picture block

TEMPLATES:
7 (A-G)

PIECES PER BLOCK:
12

Triangle A:	1 white
A(rev):	1 white
Shape B:	1 gray
B(rev):	1 gray
Triangle C:	1 white
Shape D:	1 gray
Shape E:	1 gray
E(rev):	1 gray
Shape F:	1 white
F(rev):	1 white
Shape G:	1 white
G(rev):	1 white

BLOCK ASSEMBLY:

Join long edge of A to short edge of B as shown. Repeat to join A(rev) and B(rev). Join A/B and A(rev)/B(rev) to C as shown.

Join E and E(rev) to short edges of D as shown. Join A/B/C unit to D/E unit, stitching B/E seam and B(rev)/E(rev) seam separately to leave seam allowances free-floating at center.

Set F into D/E seam line, leaving s.a. free-floating at inside corner. Set in F(rev), G, and G(rev) in same manner.

Chair Pocket

FINISHED SIZE:
12½" x 25¼"

INSTRUCTIONS:

Make 1 Sweet-Gum Leaf block, using print fabric for the gray pieces in Block Diagram. From the same print, cut 2 strips, each 1" x 10" (add s.a.), and 2 strips, each 1" x 12" (add s.a.). Join strips to edges of block as shown . Cut 12" (add s.a.) squares from white (backing) and batting.

Stack batting, block (right side up), and backing (right side down). Join along bottom edge. Turn and baste along raw edges. Quilt as desired.

Cut a 12" x 13½" (add s.a.) rectangle from print. Cut a 6¾" x 12" (add s.a) rectangle from batting. Fold fabric in half widthwise, with wrong sides facing. Insert batting in fold. Baste raw edges through all layers. Topstitch folded edge, ¼" from fold.

From white fabric, cut a 12" x 24¾" rectangle (add s.a.) and a 13" x 25¾" rectangle (add s.a.). Position sweet-gum pocket and print pocket right side up on small rectangle as shown in photo, with folded edges toward center and raw edges aligned. Baste.

Center small rectangle on large rectangle. Join rectangles, stitching ¼" inside raw edge of small rectangle. Fold edges of large rectangle forward to create a self-binding. Turn under ¼" and slip-stitch binding to front, mitering corners. To make compartments in small pocket, topstitch through all layers with a vertical seam 6½" from left edge and another seam 4" from right edge.

FABRIC REQUIREMENTS:
White: ¾ yd.
Print: ½ yd.
Batting: ⅜ yd.

Patterns are for 10" block.

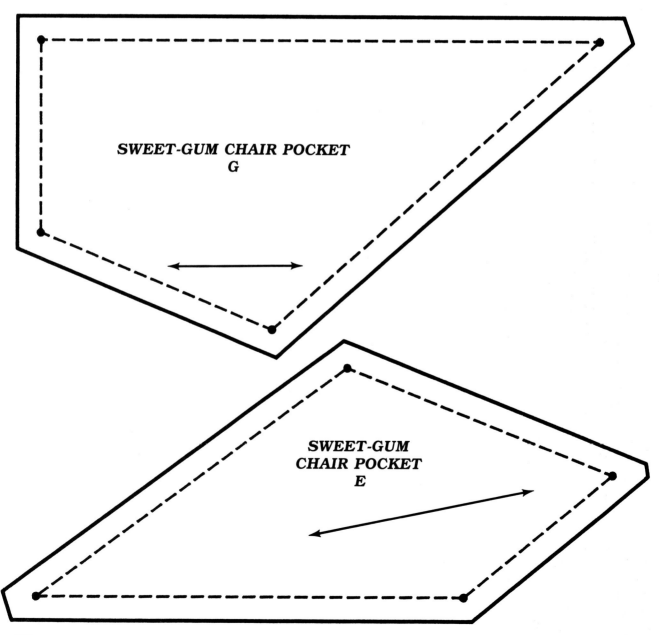

SWEET-GUM CHAIR POCKET
G

SWEET-GUM
CHAIR POCKET
E

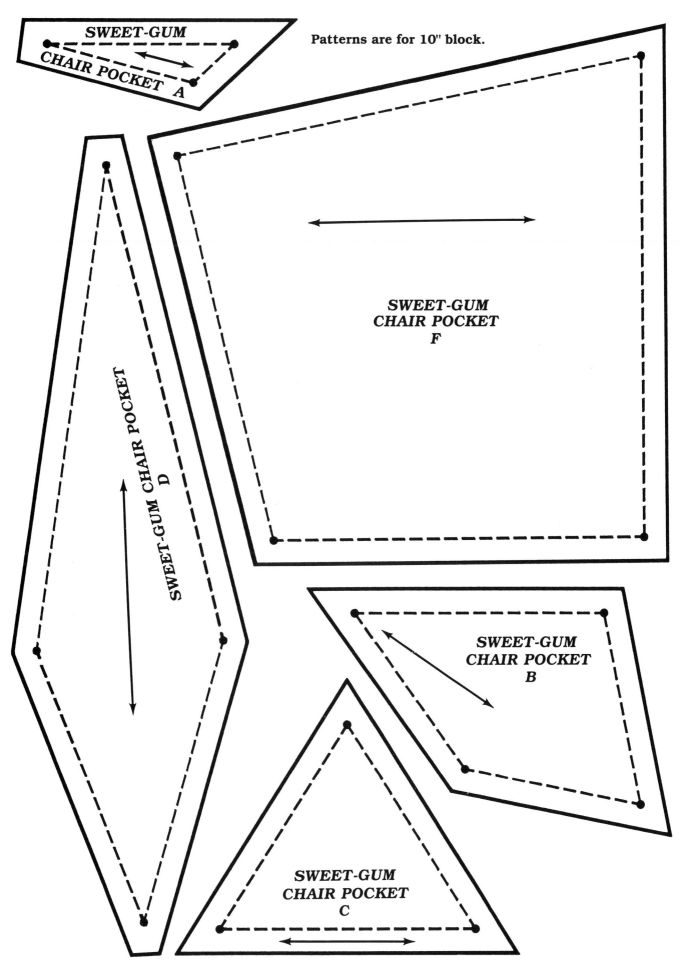

SWEET-GUM
CHAIR POCKET A

Patterns are for 10" block.

SWEET-GUM CHAIR POCKET D

SWEET-GUM
CHAIR POCKET
F

SWEET-GUM
CHAIR POCKET
B

SWEET-GUM
CHAIR POCKET
C

Fan Fire Screen

1 *One day, Georgia looked at her black, dormant fireplace and decided it needed a summertime lift. She found that the pretty paper screens she saw also came with pretty price tags. So, she thought, why not design and make her own pleated cloth coverup to decorate that open area? The result is the lovely piece you see here. It's quick to make at a reasonable cost. Repleated, it stores easily in a tube. Grid-Grip gives it stability, and a yardstick forms the base.*

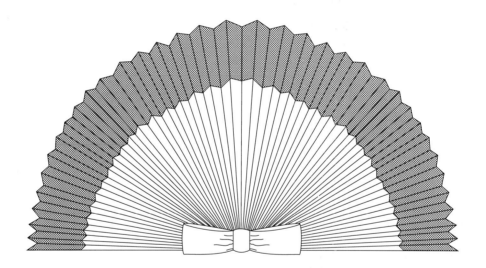

FINISHED SIZE:
18" x 36"

TYPE:
Miscellaneous

TEMPLATES:
None

Fire Screen

INSTRUCTIONS:
From striped fabric, cut 2 strips, each 5¼" x 36" (seam allowances included). (*Note:* Cut strips so that pattern will match when strips meet end to end as shown in photo.) Then cut 1 strip, 3¼" x 20½" (s.a. included), and 1 strip, 1¾" x 6½" (s.a. included). From solid fabric, cut 1 rectangle,

26½" x 36" (s.a. included); 1 strip, 3¼" x 20½" (s.a. included); and 1 strip, 1¾" x 6½" (s.a. included). From Grid-Grip, cut 2 pieces, each 18" x 36".

Remove spines from report covers. Tape spines together end to end, making sure slot remains open at the joint. Trim length of taped spine to 18".

Join 36" striped strips to opposite ends of solid fabric rectangle with ¼" seam to make a square. (See Diagram 1.) Press seams open. Iron Grid-Grip to wrong side of square, pressing hard with a hot, dry iron to stick paper to fabric. Stitch around all sides of square with a tight, narrow zigzag stitch to finish edges.

Working from Grid-Grip side and using lines on the paper as a guide, fan-fold paper-backed fabric into 1"-deep pleats, as shown in Diagram 2. Then press with warm iron to crease. Staple

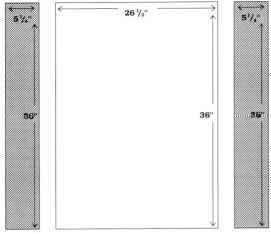

Diagram 1

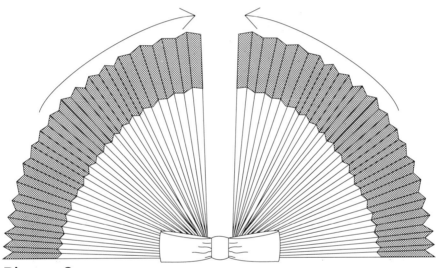

Diagram 2

Diagram 3

yardstick on wrong side of last pleat on bottom edge of square to provide a stable base for fan.

To make bow, with right sides facing and raw edges aligned, join 3¼" x 20½" solid and striped strips along long edges. Turn tube right side out, press flat, and finish ends with zigzag stitch. Whipstitch ends of strip together to form a circle. With seam centered in back, flatten circle and pinch together in center to form loops for bow; baste. For center of bow, join 1¾" x 6½" solid and striped strips, turn, press, and finish ends in same manner as for bow. Separate Velcro and sew pieces to ends of strip.

With fan folded, place bow at center on right side of pleated fabric and wrap small strip around bow and fan, securing ends with Velcro. Unfold fan, bringing top edges of pleated fabric together at center, as shown in Diagram 3. Slide plastic spine over fabric edges where they meet

on back of fan to join edges securely while fan is in use. (Remove spine and collapse fan for easy storage.)

FABRIC AND NOTIONS REQUIREMENTS:
Vertical-stripe border fabric: 1⅛ yd.
Solid fabric: 1⅛ yd.
2 (18" x 36") pieces of Grid-Grip (or freezer paper with 1" grid drawn on it)
2 report covers with sliding plastic spines (available from office-supply stores)
Masking tape
Wooden yardstick
Stapler
1 (½" x 1") piece of Velcro

Spinning Spools Quilts

*Beautiful quilts—that's what quilters
love most, and the Spinning Spools Pattern
Club is full of photographs and drawings of
exciting quilt designs, each with full
instructions included.*

*In this sampler booklet, you'll find
instructions for three Spinning Spools quilts.
I designed the Spinning Spools Star
especially to celebrate
the beginning of the pattern club.
The stretched Spools pattern, one of my
favorite designs, is set spinning in this quilt
to form a glorious spools star.*

*The Pomegranates quilt, its design
taken from a quilt in the collection of the
Tennessee State Museum, is our homage to the
beauty of traditional patterns. Use this pattern
to perfect your appliqué skills.*

*Georgia's Club Sandwich combines
twenty of the blocks from this booklet.
In making this quilt, you'll learn how to
combine blocks of different sizes
into one dazzling sampler.*

Spinning Spools Star

The Spools pattern is a favorite of mine. In my books, I've explored many variations of this interesting design. Here's my brand new interpretation of the pattern, in which the "stretched" spools come together in a whirling star.

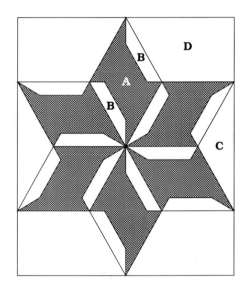

Block

FINISHED SIZE:
12" x 14"

TYPE:
Diamonds

TEMPLATES:
4 (A-D)

PIECES PER BLOCK:
24

Shape A:	6 gray
Trapezoid B:	12 white
Triangle C:	2 white
Shape D:	2 white
D(rev):	2 white

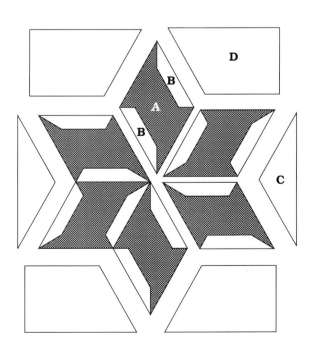

BLOCK ASSEMBLY:

Set 2 pieces B into each A piece to form spool units. (To machine-stitch this, first join B to A along the long straight edge, back-stitching at each turning dot. Clip the obtuse angles and then stitch outward, aligning raw edges at each corner. Press seams inward toward the spool.)

When all 6 spool units have been made, join them together, one at a time, to make a star. (You can hand-piece the spools together, one at a time, up to the center point, which allows quarter-inch seam allowances to spiral around center point. Or, you can machine-stitch 3 stars and then another 3 stars, stagger the seam allowances, and stitch the 2 halves together.)

Set 1 C piece into each side of star. Join 4 D pieces to fill corners. Sew up to the quarter-inch mark, always leaving free-floating seam allowances.

Wall Hanging

FINISHED SIZE:
44" x 49"

SETTING:

To make this continuous setting, first make 8 stars and 2 half-stars (plus 4 separate spools for corners of borders).

When you set the stars together as shown in our quilt photograph, the spaces between them become hexagons. To make the pattern for this hexagon, make longest stitching line of template D into a fold line, doubling the size of D. Then add triangle C (omitting seam allowances where you overlap pattern pieces) to complete the hexagon. Ten full hexagons are required.

Set stars together, with hexagons between, as shown. Sew up to the quarter-inch mark, always leaving free-floating seam allowances. Fill side edges with 4 pieces made with template D, reversed to double its size, and place regular Ds in corners (2 sets of mirror images). To fill top and bottom edges, cut four special Ds, which are one half of the full hexagon with a seam allowance added on the long side.

BORDERS:

To make inner side borders, cut 2 trapezoids from plaid or striped fabric, each 2" wide, 35" along shorter edge, and 42" along longer edge (add seam allowances to all edges). Cut 2 same-size outer side borders from floral print. Join 1 plaid to 1 floral trapezoid along shorter edges for each side border. Set a single spool unit, for a corner block, into each end of each border.

To make inner top and bottom borders, cut 2 trapezoids from plaid or striped fabric, each 2" wide, 36" along shorter edge, and 38¼" along longer edge (add seam allowances to all edges).

For outer top and bottom borders, cut 2 floral trapezoids, each 1½" wide, 38¼" along shorter edge, and 40" along longer edge (add seam allowances to all edges). Join 1 plaid trapezoid to 1 floral trapezoid, as shown, to make top border. Repeat for bottom border. Set top and bottom borders in, joining to top and bottom edges of quilt and to corner spools.

FABRIC REQUIREMENTS:
White: ⅝ yd.
Shape A: 2 yd., or, if multicolored spools are desired, ⅝ yd. each of 3 different colors.
Plaid: ⅓ yd.
Floral print: 1½ yd.

Quilting Option: Dotted lines are machine-stitched; broken lines are hand-stitched.

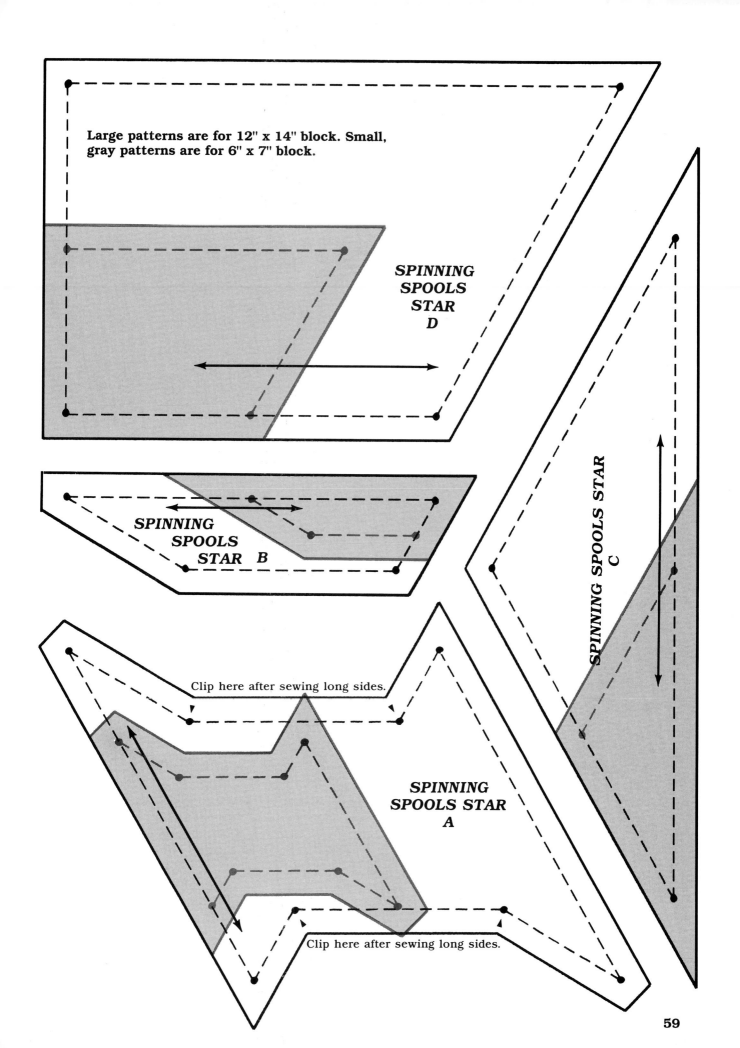

Large patterns are for 12" x 14" block. Small, gray patterns are for 6" x 7" block.

SPINNING
SPOOLS
STAR
D

SPINNING
SPOOLS
STAR B

SPINNING SPOOLS STAR
C

Clip here after sewing long sides.

SPINNING
SPOOLS STAR
A

Clip here after sewing long sides.

Pomegranates

3 *At first glance, you may miss the basic block of this pomegranate quilt—stems grow from the corners of the block with pomegranates toward the center. It's only when the blocks are joined that the four stems appear to branch from a central axis. Each stem-and-pomegranate motif is first pieced and then appliquéd to the background. The large motif and its high contrast to the background call for a bold border, and a tricolor stripe tipped with piping fills the bill. Quilting is in contour lines on and around the plant shapes and in a diagonal grid on the background.*

Block

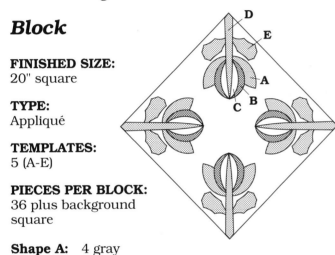

FINISHED SIZE:
20" square

TYPE:
Appliqué

TEMPLATES:
5 (A-E)

PIECES PER BLOCK:
36 plus background
square

Shape A:	4 gray			
A(rev):	4 gray			
Shape B:	4 dark gray	**Shape D:**	4 gray
B(rev):	4 dark gray	**Shape E:**	4 gray
Shape C:	4 white	**E(rev):**	4 gray

BLOCK ASSEMBLY:

Join A to B, matching corner dot at upper right corner of A to dot on seam line of B. Stitch from bottom edge of A to upper right A corner dot and backstitch, leaving A/B seam allowances free-floating above dot. Join B to C as shown.

Join A/B/C unit to left side of D, matching lower A corner dot to dot on D seam line and leaving s.a. free-floating below dot. Repeat to join A(rev)/B(rev)/C(rev) unit to right side of D. Join E and E(rev) units to D, matching corner dots on E and E(rev) to dots on D and leaving s.a. free-floating. Repeat to piece 3 more pomegranates.

Cut a 20" square (add s.a.) of muslin with bias edges (so that the straight-of-grain runs through the diagonal center of the block). Mark diagonal center lines. Turn under ¼" s.a. around top and sides of 1 pomegranate and press or baste to secure. Center pomegranate on fold line in 1 quadrant of square as shown, matching base of stem with corner of square. Repeat to position remaining pomegranates. Appliqué pomegranates to square.

Quilt

FINISHED SIZE:
97" square

SETTING:

Make 13 blocks as shown above. Cut 2 squares from muslin, each 29½" x 29½" (s.a. included). Cut each square diagonally into quarters to make a total of 8 (20⅞") setting triangles. Make and appliqué 1 pomegranate to each of these setting triangles as shown. Cut 2 squares from muslin, each 15" x 15" (s.a. included). Cut each square diagonally in half to make a total of 4 corner triangles.

Join setting triangles, corner triangles, and blocks in diagonal rows, referring to Quilt Diagram for placement. Join rows.

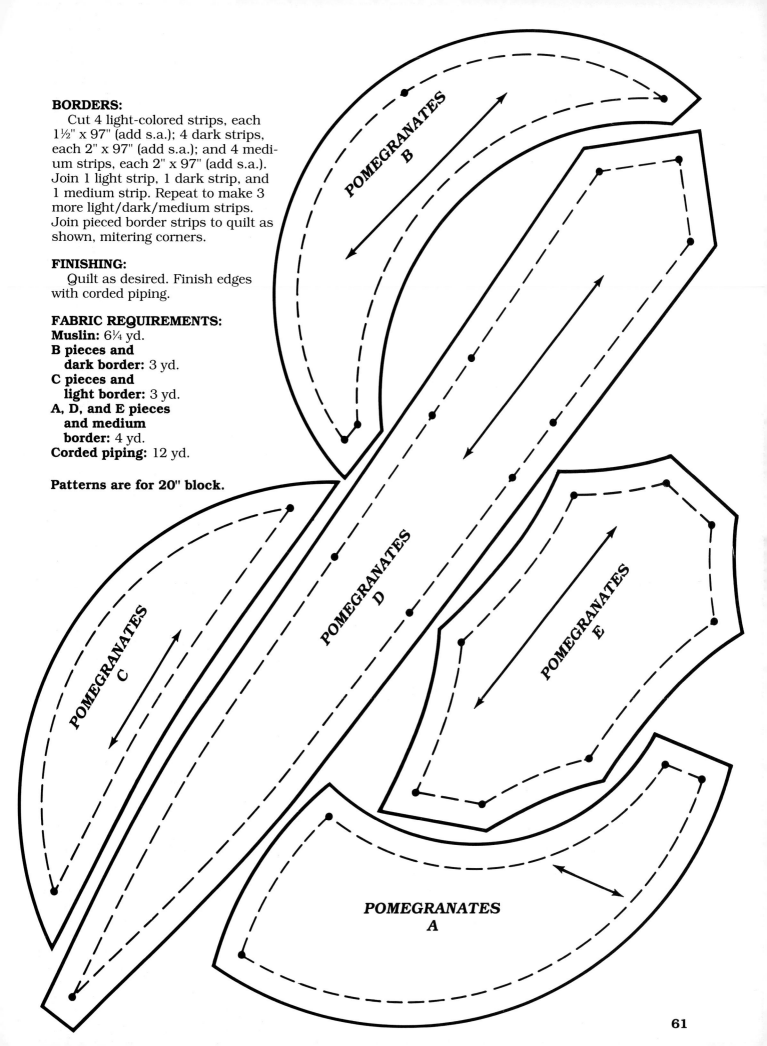

BORDERS:
Cut 4 light-colored strips, each 1½" x 97" (add s.a.); 4 dark strips, each 2" x 97" (add s.a.); and 4 medium strips, each 2" x 97" (add s.a.). Join 1 light strip, 1 dark strip, and 1 medium strip. Repeat to make 3 more light/dark/medium strips. Join pieced border strips to quilt as shown, mitering corners.

FINISHING:
Quilt as desired. Finish edges with corded piping.

FABRIC REQUIREMENTS:
Muslin: 6¼ yd.
B pieces and dark border: 3 yd.
C pieces and light border: 3 yd.
A, D, and E pieces and medium border: 4 yd.
Corded piping: 12 yd.

Patterns are for 20" block.

POMEGRANATES B

POMEGRANATES D

POMEGRANATES C

POMEGRANATES E

POMEGRANATES A

Georgia's Club Sandwich

3 To join a variety of odd-sized Spinning Spools blocks into one sampler quilt, Georgia added a colorful floral print and Flying Geese strips as needed to make all her blocks uniform 18-inch squares. The success of this quilt lies in the arrangement of blocks. Before beginning assembly, lay out your blocks and shuffle them to determine the most pleasing balance of color and pattern.

The placement of the Flying Geese motif (which appears in two different sizes) is especially important because the pattern is so graphic. In piecing Flying Geese, Georgia advises, "Using the master template really helps here so that you don't lose the right-angle points of each formation."

FINISHED SIZE:
18" square

TYPE:
Pieced and appliquéd

TEMPLATES:
6 (A-F) (**Note:** Use these templates to construct pieced border strips to enlarge blocks to standard size. Refer to individual block instructions for remaining templates.)

BLOCK ASSEMBLY:
Make 20 sampler blocks as shown in Assembly Diagram. Refer to templates and block instructions given earlier in this booklet.

1A: 12" Joseph's Coat
1B: 15" Mother's Dream
1C: 12" Old Maid's Puzzle
1D: 12" Shaded Trail
1E: 12" Bear's Paw
2A: 12" Flying Dutchman
2B: 18" Flying Swallows
2C: 15" Wheels
2D: 16" Oak Leaf & Reel
2E: 12" Indian Meadows
3A: 12" Pinwheel
3B: 16" Fancy Dresden Plate
3C: 12" Star of Bethlehem
(**Note:** Rotate block ¼ turn.)
3D: 14" Old-Fashioned Nosegay
3E: 12" Double Attic Windows
4A: 12" Tall Pine Tree
4B: 12" Weather Vane
4C: 15" Burgoyne Surrounded
4D: 12" Crazy Cats
(**Note:** This is an enlarged version of the original 10" block; simply make a larger foundation block.)
4E: 12" Missouri Star

Quilt

FINISHED SIZE:
78" x 96" (including 3" ruffle)

SETTING:
From coordinating multicolored floral print, cut strips as follows, adding ¼" seam allowances to each: 8 (6" x 18"), 10 (6" x 12"), 2 (4" x 18"), 3 (3" x 18"), 1 (3" x 15"), 2 (2" x 18"), and 2 (2" x 16"). (**Note:** These strips will be used to enlarge smaller blocks to 18" x 18" size.) From same fabric, cut 84 Bs and 44 Es.

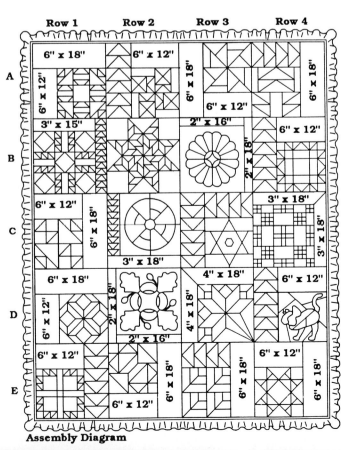

Assembly Diagram

From second print, cut 2 squares, each 16" x 16" (add s.a.) to use as background for appliqués. Cut 6"-wide (add s.a.) bias strips, piecing as needed to equal 20 yards for making ruffle.

From black, cut 42 As and 22 Ds. Also from black, cut ½"-wide (add s.a.) bias strips, piecing as needed to equal 11 yards for facing. From black, cut ¾"-wide (s.a. included) bias strips, piecing as needed to equal 11 yards for corded piping. With cording, make corded piping.

To make Flying Geese, join 2 print Bs to short edges of 1 black A. Repeat to make 41 more A/B rectangles. Use template C as a guide to trim rectangles to uniform size. Join rectangles as shown in photograph to make 5 (6-unit) strips and 3 (4-unit) strips.

Repeat to make 22 D/E rectangles. Use template F to trim rectangles to uniform size. Join rectangles to make 1 (10-unit) and 1 (12-unit) strip.

Join print and pieced strips to blocks as shown in Assembly Diagram to make all blocks the same size. Join blocks as shown to make 4 (5-block) vertical rows.

Lap-quilt rows separately and join, using the lap-quilting connection. (***Note:*** Refer to pages 3–6 for quilting options.)

FINISHING:

With wrong sides facing and raw edges aligned, fold ruffle strip in half lengthwise. Gather to fit perimeter of quilt. With raw edges aligned, stack quilt (right side up), corded piping, ruffle, and bias facing strip (right side down). Join. Fold facing strip to back of quilt, turn under ¼" s.a. on raw edge, and slipstitch to back to finish edges.

FABRIC AND NOTION REQUIREMENTS:
Floral print: 2½ yd.
Second print: 4 yd.
Black: 1⅛ yd.
¼" cording: 11 yd.

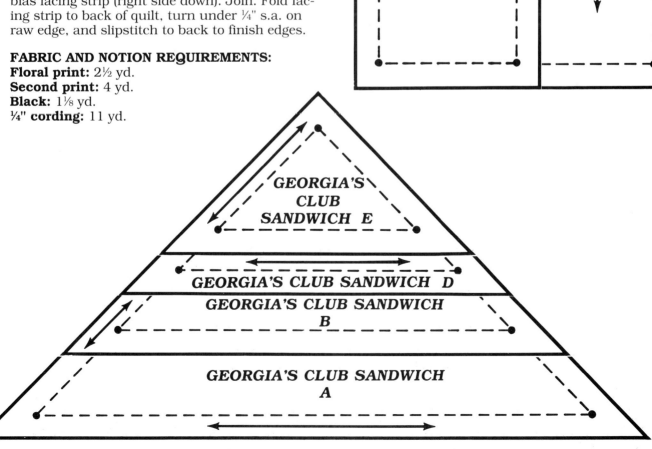

Use these master templates to check Flying Geese units.

GEORGIA'S CLUB SANDWICH
C

GEORGIA'S CLUB SANDWICH F

GEORGIA'S CLUB SANDWICH E

GEORGIA'S CLUB SANDWICH D

GEORGIA'S CLUB SANDWICH B

GEORGIA'S CLUB SANDWICH A

Join *GEORGIA BONESTEEL'S* best-selling pattern club for creative quilters like you!

SPINNING SPOOLS: A Pattern Club for Quilters is an exciting way to keep up-to-date on Georgia's newest quilt finds and to share her latest quilting tips and techniques. Her PBS series and the *Spinning Spool Sampler* feature only a few specially selected patterns from her collection. As a member of the club, you'll have a chance to preview the whole collection and to join Georgia in her continuing search for the world's finest quilts, both heirloom and original.

*N*obody knows quilting like Georgia!

She's published books on quilting. She's been the guest at scores of quilting clubs. She continues to host her own PBS television series. And, because she revolutionized the world of quilting with her concept of LAP QUILTING, she's known as the *First Lady of Lap Quilting.* Now, as a member of **SPINNING SPOOLS**, you can reap the benefits of her knowledge and her distinctive flair for quilting on a regular basis in your own home.

When you join **SPINNING SPOOLS**, you will receive the gifts descibed above, **PLUS** a second *PatternPak* to look over for 30 days. If you decide to keep the second *PatternPak*, you will

Templates galore and a whole lot more!
Join now as a charter member and you'll get:

FREE! A *PatternPak*™ of full-size templates, patterns and instructions for making 3 beautiful quilts!

FREE! A colorful, laminated 9" x 12" binder to keep your patterns and templates at hand!

FREE! 12 Index Dividers to help you file— and— find your patterns fast!

Free! Volume 1 of Georgia's **SPINNING SPOOLS NEWSLETTER** brimming with the latest news of Georgia's teaching and travels, plus a column for readers to share ideas, patterns, quilting tips and more!

PLUS, you'll get a second *Patternpak* of templates and patterns to look over for 30 days free!

pay only the low rate of $5.98, plus shipping and handling. Then about every month you will receive a shipment of two brand new *PatternPaks* and a copy of Georgia's latest newsletter. You'll always have 30 days to decide to keep or return a shipment. And you may cancel anytime. That's all there is to it. The free gifts are yours to keep — forever!

*M*ore good news! When you do join **SPINNING SPOOLS**, you'll receive this distinctive club pin designed by Georgia herself!

If you think SPINNING SPOOLS is for you, join the club by calling us toll free any day, anytime
1·800·765·6400

If you would like to reinstate your membership in SPINNING SPOOLS, call toll free Monday thru Friday
1·800·633·4910

Oxmoor House®

P.O. Box 2463 Birmingham, Al 35201